Lynn Jericho

Six Ways To

Celebrate Christmas!

&

Celebrate You!

An *Inner Christmas* Book

An *Inner Christmas* Book
PO Box 732
Chatham, NJ 07928
www.InnerChristmas.com

Jericho, Lynn, 1947–
Six Ways To Celebrate Christmas! & Celebrate You! / Lynn
  Jericho
ISBN 0-9723312-6-3

I always appreciate it when folks write and ask permission to quote my work. I always give it.

I request that you give me credit for any work of mine that you use, and ideally, provide a link back to the original.

I am available for lectures, workshops, and interviews on Inner Christmas, the Inner Year and many other topics. I get my greatest inspirations from my audiences. Please contact me via email.

I apologize for any typos; please let me know if you find any so I can correct them. If you do not understand something and need some clarification, please email me.

Lynn Jericho
www.innerchristmas.com
lynnjericho@gmail.com

Dedication

To the founding faculty, families, and friends
of the Waldorf School of Princeton.

Contents

Author's Note

Dear Reader,

I want to share with you why you will want to read this book and why I wrote it.

If you want more than a merry Christmas, if you also want a meaningful Christmas, you will find *Six Ways To Celebrate Christmas! & Celebrate You!* an inspiring book. I write about the meaning of Christmas, and about the ways *your soul renews its own meaning* at Christmas time.

Celebrate comes from a Latin word for honoring. Today we don't use the verb "honor" very often. Yet, we can imagine how different our world would be if we, each one of us on the planet, had been asked every day in school and at the dinner table to share what we honored—not told what to honor, but asked. Honoring lives naturally in our souls, but it must be awakened and exercised to encourage both reverence and blessing in our relationships to all things material and spiritual. Honoring can't be taught, but it can be modeled.

This little book seeks to awaken and exercise your soul to what it honors and celebrates at Christmas.

In searching my own soul I found six distinct Christmas celebrations where I honored particular relationships in my life. My Christmas celebrations honor:

Nature and the cycle of the Sun as reflected in the cycle of my soul

Nativity and the (re)birth of the innocent Divine within my soul

Riches and the sensuous delights of my material existence

Relationships and the presence of my family, friends and community

Childhood and the powerful impact of my early memories on my present Christmas

Selfhood and my emerging, evolving sense of self

Six Ways To Celebrate Christmas! & Celebrate You! intends to help you find the ways your soul, your personal humanity, finds more inner depth, inner height and inner breadth in and through the six experiences of Christmas. Christmas is the time of year that both spirit and matter, both the heavenly and the earthly, come together to awaken the ways you honor your sense of self, your sense of others, your sense of our planet, your sense of the divine and your sense of the future.

Six Ways To Celebrate Christmas! & Celebrate You! asks you to think and contemplate on the many ways you find inner benefit, clarity and meaning during Christmas. The book offers questions and guidance for enriching your own Christmas experience and celebration.

Before you begin the book, I want to explore, perhaps illuminate, some important thoughts on what I feel limits our ability to have the most fulfilling Christmas celebrations. First, I will address sentimentality and cynicism, the two feelings that get in the way of honoring the potential for personal growth during the holiday. Secondly, I want to share a bit about stages of consciousness that influence how we experience Christmas.

SENTIMENTALITY AND CYNICISM

Sentimentality is not meaning. It is nostalgia. Sentimental Christmas' feelings rise out of your past Christmases or out of emotional longings and fantasies about how you wish Christmas could, should or would be. A merry Christmas can be full of sentiment and offer much enjoyment. However, sentimental feelings can also keep us emotionally stuck in Christmases Past or Future, unable to appreciate Christmas Present. Be aware of your sentimental feelings and keep them in balance. *Six Ways To Celebrate Christmas! & Celebrate You!* does not intend to increase or decrease your sentimental Christmas' feelings but intends to free you from dependence on sentiment during the holidays.

Cynicism doubts value, meaning, and purpose. A lot of people have cynical feelings about parts of Christmas. In general, cynicism questions either the material aspects or the spiritual aspects of Christmas. Christmas cynicism can be a limiting prejudice or it can be a liberating questioning. *Six Ways To Celebrate Christmas! & Celebrate You!* is about questioning, not prejudice.

I am both sentimental and cynical about many aspects of Christmas. This book is a result of my sentimental memories and longings and my cynical concerns about the apparent lack of meaning, value and purpose in my Christmas traditions and experiences. Sentimentality and cynicism are great door openers to insight and inspiration.

As you work with the six imaginations of Christmas, pay attention to your sentimentality and your cynicism about each one. I suggest you write down both your sentimental feelings and your cynical feelings about each Christmas experience. (A working journal is available at www.innerchristmas.com/store.) Be truthful. If you want to inwardly evolve your thoughts, feelings and intentions, you want to confront your sentimental attachments and your cynical doubts. Ask yourself, "How is my Christmas experience and my inner development served by this sentiment? Or this cynicism?" I am certain you will find surprising benefit from consciously observing and exploring your sentimentality and your cynicism. Use the insights on each of six Christmases to guide your exploration.

LEVELS OF CONSCIOUSNESS

All great researchers of human consciousness and human freedom recognize levels of awareness or consciousness. As I pay attention to myself and to others with growing compassion, I find having a sense of these levels of awareness, being able to name them and observing how quickly and innocently we move from one level to another in any circumstance, offers more vibrant knowledge of my evolving individuality. The levels are more like layers that form a whole experience and should not be seen as separate and hierarchical in value.

In the course of any Christmas celebration, I can be at any one level of consciousness. My experience can be at the level of consciousness shaped by my memories of being 5 years old. I can be focused on having an experience shaped by my family and my Protestant upbringing. I can be totally immersed in the sensory delights of materialistic indulgences. I can be in a dreamlike state of spiritual awe. And so on...

Consciously, I can be fully awake to the level of my experience. I can be dreamily, vaguely sensitive to it. Or, I can be in the deep sleep of no awareness. As I wrote this book, I spent much time waking myself up, not in the moment but in recollection. I would recall my Christmas experiences and imagine being awake and aware to the surface experiences, the hidden, underlying meaning of the experience and my own sentimentality and cynicism regarding the experience.

Also, I work to be awake to my goals for Christmas. I bring my vague longings to clear declarations. I write down my intentions and address how to bring them into reality. I bring consciousness to my thoughts, my feelings and

Author's Note

my essential actions. What do I want? Why do I want it? What do I need to do to make it happen?

I want you to wake up to Christmas and the meaning you find in the six ways you can celebrate the holiday. Use my questions to wake yourself up.

If you are interested in "waking up" to levels of consciousness, if you want to understand your experiences and find more freedom in your participation in life, here are some great resources that give brief and easy to understand imaginations of levels of consciousness:

http://www.newlightbeings.com/
   video/1807389:Video:3313

http://chedal.blogspot.com/2008/03/synopsis-integral-
   conciousness-and.html

http://the-mouse-trap.blogspot.com/2008/09/robert-
   kegans-stages-of-social-maturity.html

WHEN AND HOW TO READ THIS BOOK

First, read *Six Ways To Celebrate Christmas! & Celebrate You!* during the year. You may have bought this book at Christmas time and you can certainly read it at Christmas but I suggest you read this book at another time of year. What you read and how to respond to what you read will change your sense of what you want in and from your Christmas experience.

Probably, the best time to read this book is when you first start to anticipate the next Christmas. For some of us that is December 26th. For others, it is some late summer day when something in the air or the shape of the clouds in the sky announces the season will soon change. Or you may find the book perfect for early December.

Give yourself time to read this book. It is a book that asks you to spend about ten times as much time contemplating the ideas and questions as reading them. This is why I wrote a short book. It's really not short. It is really a very long book, but most of the book is being written by you in your own inner work. You are my co-author.

Please read this with a journal and a pen. Write down your "aha's." Write down your questions. Write down your impulses. Write down your ideas and ideals for your Christmas celebrations. Write down the things you want to discuss with your family, your friends, your spiritual mentors.

Create your own Celebrate Christmas! Cel-

Author's Note

ebrate Me! book. Use the *Six Ways To Celebrate Christmas! & Celebrate You! Working Journal* for your imaginations, or use your own journal. Re-read your version of the book and re-write it every year.

WHY I WROTE THIS BOOK...

Here I will make some declarations about myself. I will try to be transparent and authentic. I am writing a book that intends to evolve or change your thoughts, your feelings and your actions about Christmas. You need to know a bit about me. On my web site www.innerchristmas.com there is an audio file where I answer a number of questions I found on the site for the Center for Media Literacy http://www.medialit.org/bp_mlk.html. Media literacy occurs when you begin to consider the message and the message maker.

You are reading a message I made. Below are some things I want you to know about me. If you want to know more, email me at lynnjericho@ gmail.com.

In the best light on my best days I can say the following:

I am a spiritual seeker. I seek the spirit in all things. I seek the truth, the beauty and the goodness in all human endeavor, in thoughts, feelings and deeds.

No matter how frustrated and resentful I felt at Christmas, I always sought the Christmas spirit. It took years find and articulate the Christmas spirit in my thoughts. I wrote this book to share what I have found. What I have written should point you in some fruitful directions. I do assume you are a seeker, too.

And I am a striver. I strive to be better, more congruent, more coherent, more cohesive and more creative. Paradoxically, I must often become more chaotic first.

I've had some pretty chaotic Christmases as I strove to have a better Christmas. I usually didn't have the right questions to get to the right answers about what "better" actually was. I have included lots of questions to help you clarify your Christmas striving.

By asking myself a lot of questions, I realized there were these six distinct Christmases, but they all have been collapsed into one amorphous Christmas. By "de-collapsing" Christmas, I discovered Christmas congruence, coherence, cohesiveness and creativity. I broke Christmas into parts so it could all come together, beautifully.

Yes, you can have a better Christmas, a better six distinct Christmases each year. Let Christmas evolve as you evolve.

I am a "meaning junkie." I always want to get to the meaning of something, so I think a lot. If a thought, a feeling or a deed, doesn't have meaning ... what's the point? Meaning must ring true for me *in freedom*. I cannot deal with dogma, religious, political or personal. Once something becomes dogma it has lost spiritual meaning and only exists to control and deny freedom.

I always squirmed at the religious and commercial dogma about Christmas. I did not want to conform to an outside authority on Christmas. Nor did I want to hang one more ornament or sing one more Christmas song or have one more Christmas conversation, without knowing the purpose, significance or meaning behind it.

Over many Christmases, I would go into my Christmas meaning quest for a few moments several times a day from the moment I saw the first Christmas decoration in a store or on a street in early November. The quest would peak the week before Christmas and last until Christmas night, when it would go away for

10 months. Once I began *Inner Christmas* and began getting so much appreciation for my efforts—Christmas and all its meanings became a year long focus.

I wrote *Six Ways To Celebrate Christmas! & Celebrate You!* so you could find your Christmas meaning and Christmas freedom. You will need to do more than read my words. You will need to answer my questions and the questions that arise in your own soul with each Christmas. Love questions because they get you to your meaning. Then question the meaning.

I love design and art. I majored in art history and worked as an interior designer.

Art and design are about creating beautiful, meaningful images and relationships. I wrote this book to awaken and empower the Christmas artist and designer in you. You can create the Christmas that your soul imagines and needs.

I am a co-healer. I see hurts and wounds, suffering and sickness, and excesses and deficiencies everywhere. I see the potential for healing, restoring and renewing in the many aspects of Christmas.

I believe most of us need Christmas healing. I wrote this book to help you self-heal. We all desire and deserve a healthy Christmas every year.

I wrote this book as a guide to finding the truth, beauty and goodness of your Christmas experiences. I wrote this book to heal your Christmas soul; to liberate your Christmas soul and to strengthen your Christmas soul.

I ask a lot of questions and offer a lot of perspectives. As a guide it is meant to serve your soul for many Christmases. You may want to bring your creative attention to just one of the first five Christmases each year. Let your awakening to Christmas meaning and Christmas healing unfold slowly.

The Christmas of Selfhood is a celebration you can begin this year. Join thousands of others working with the *Inner Christmas* messages during the Twelve Holy Nights by subscribing at www.innerchristmas.com. The yearly *Inner Christmas* messages are my Christmas gift to all my fellow human souls.

My Ultimate Christmas Wish for You

I want you to find love in Christmas, in each of the six Christmases. I want you to love Nature. I want you to love the innocent Divine in your soul. I want you to love all the expressions of material riches. I want you to love all those who share life with you. I want you to love all the early memories that shape your emotions and desires at Christmas. I want you to love your inner development as an evolving individual.

Love is goodwill and from goodwill we find the blessing of peace. Christmas is the time of year we celebrate our ability to love and to bring goodwill into our own lives and into the world.

Celebrate Christmas! Celebrate You!

Introduction

Introduction

CHRISTMAS QUESTIONS AND CHRISTMAS REACTIONS

Christmas is the most complex time of year for our souls. Inwardly, we struggle with all kinds of feelings, intentions, capacities and limitations. The Christmas complexities and struggles show up in my soul as questions and reactions.

Every year the same questions and a few new ones. I am usually too busy to find any answers so the questions persist. My inner Christmas questions are just another Christmas tradition, a box of inner Christmas ornaments I bring down from the attic in my soul every year with the rest of the Christmas stuff. Some of my dominating Christmas questions are:

What do I want *for* Christmas and *from* Christmas?

What does Christmas *really mean* to me?

How do I manage being Santa, Martha Stewart and the Virgin Mary all at once? And still be me?

Why does the unredeemed Scrooge hide in my soul letting out little bits of Christmas resistance and resentment every now and then?

How do I bring love and joy to the Little Matchgirl in my soul that never feels she can join the Christmas party?

Do I have any real connection to the spiritual significance of Christmas?

What about the New Year? Will it really be new? Will I really be new?

These are great questions and deserve to be given answers. The answers will inspire a new Christmas, a Christmas that would bear wonderful gifts of meaning for my soul.

I also have a set of reactions to the many aspects of Christmas:

> awe and awful,
>
> delight and disappointment,
>
> enthusiasm and exhaustion,
>
> blessings,
>
> blues,
>
> blahs,
>
> *and bah humbugs.*

My spiritual reaction is either "awe or awful." Awful is an aesthetic response to the portrayal of the Nativity story in plastic art, music and the media. Awe comes from great music and great paintings and the natural world. A beautiful Christmas landscape and the Christmas sky filled with stars can take my breath away.

Decorations, gifts and foods bring delight or disappointment. I also find delight in the Christmas presence of family and friends and disappointment in their absence.

Enthusiasm and exhaustion reflect my physical and emotional well-being and energy levels. Do I sense that the outcome will be worth the effort? Do I have a clear picture of what I want to make or do? How overwhelmed am I by expectations, my own and others'?

Blessings are measured by gratitude for seeing the commonplace glowing with the special light of the season and the surprise of tender moments of meaning, beauty and love.

Blues come from associations to the past, grief over loss, unfulfilled expectations and, sometimes, just my chemistry going out of balance from over-stimulation or too much sugar.

Blahs and Bah Humbugs are my response to

tacky commercialism. Sometimes I can redeem my reactions with humor, but usually I just turn away with boredom or irritation.

I have generalized my reactions here and not made a list of specific responses to specific experiences. Keeping a Christmas reaction journal from the moment you begin to pay attention to the holiday to the moment you've put away the last string of lights and eaten the last Christmas cookie, will help you define and shape your Christmas celebrations in the future. You will find clarity about the specifics of your Christmas experience. You will develop a calm and creative response to all that Christmas brings into your life and your soul.

CHRISTMAS AND YOUR SOUL

Now that you have a clearer sense of your questions and your reactions, we can look at how this holiday shapes our souls and our years.

Regardless of our beliefs and our culture, we confront and relate to Christmas every year if only in the media and on Main Street. Most of us find our Christmas experience externally in our homes, our towns, our workplaces, our wallets and our waistlines. Internally, we find Christmas in our beliefs, our emotions, our wishes and our dreams.

There are those of us who refuse to celebrate or participate in any Christmas traditions, yet, outwardly and inwardly, we still, unwillingly, engage with the Christmas experience. Why?

The Season of Christmas has been part of our lives since we were born and a part of human consciousness since before civilization. We didn't choose it. Like the sun and the stars, Christmas is just there year after year. We may have strong feelings about Christmas—what we like and don't like, love or hate—but we have a hard time being objective enough about Christmas to have a true understanding of what it means to us and why we have such strong feelings about the holiday.

What is most clear is that the complexity of activities, feelings and desires needs to be distinguished, sorted and arranged to bring to our souls the clearest and most fulfilling personal Christmas.

Making distinctions can provide so much insight when confronting the multilayered complexity of Christmas feelings. We often collapse or muddle together very distinct and separate realities, experiences, feelings and events. By "de-collapsing" Christmas and distinguishing the six ways we experience and celebrate Christmas, we find the Christmas clarity that allows us to celebrate in freedom this amazing time of year and this amazing inner experience. The six distinctions will help us find answers to our questions and understand our reactions.

Let's begin with recognizing the three contexts of Christmas.

THE THREE CONTEXTS OF CHRISTMAS

We human beings live with a consciousness of three contexts—the cosmic, the social, and the personal. More than any other holiday, Christmas offers our souls the opportunity to engage, celebrate and find meaning in all three contexts.

The *cosmic* context of Christmas asks us to consider deep existential realities of birth and death, of Gods and Stars, of innocence and wisdom. We reflect on the soul's reflection of the great powers of Nature and the cycle of the Sun through the year. We recognize the soul's experience of the Nativity and birth of the Divine within our own human soul. This Christmas context discovers the cosmic archetypes of the universal harmony of the Cosmos reflected in Nature and the universal love of the Cosmos made evident in the Infant Jesus and the kernel of the Divine living in every human soul.

The *social* context of Christmas asks us to create environments and activities for our senses and to awaken loving sensitivities to other human beings. This Christmas context transforms our spaces, enriches our sense perceptions and nurtures our feeling of community and intimacy.

The *personal* context of Christmas asks us to reflect on our memories, our needs and our intentions for the future. We find a deep understanding of the impact of our first Christmases. We look at Christmas as an opportunity to deepen our own inner development. Through the personal Christmases, we find our own biographical relationship to Christmases Past and focus on who we are and who we are becoming as we move toward Christmases Future.

Within each of these three contexts Christmas allows us, encourages us, to engage with both our innocence and our wisdom and find both comfort and challenge during the holidays. Innocence invites us to wonder with extraordinary openness. Innocence keeps our souls tender and receptive to the comforting aspects of Christmas. Wisdom empowers our souls to uncover the challenges of inner truth and the potential for inner growth living in Christmas. Our souls need to be both comforted and challenged to move forward in our lives with renewed strength and meaning—to be new in the New Year.

To participate in Christmas without wonder and wisdom is to reduce all that lives in our souls to habit, sentiment and superficiality. Without wonder and wisdom in our souls, and our lives, we find one year moving into the next as if life is merely routine and not a mysterious and miraculous journey.

Truthfully, we have lacked a guide for our inner life at Christmas. There has been no imaginative structure on which to build a meaningful awareness of the inner gifts of Christmas. Understanding and defining the six experiences of Christmas that come each year brings cosmic, social and personal structure to our inner life and reveals the deep significance in our Christmas traditions.

My description of each of these Christmas experiences is just an introduction. You will find many more personal nuances as you consider and contemplate what lives in your own soul at Christmas time.

The six ways our souls honor Christmas are:

- *The Christmas of Nature*
  when we celebrate the exquisite harmo-
  nies living in the natural world.

- *The Christmas of Nativity*
  when we celebrate the meaning of the
  Birth of the Divine within our souls.

- *The Christmas of Riches*
  when we celebrate the sensory delights
  of our earthly lives

- *The Christmas of Relationships*
  when our hearts open up to our family,
  friends and strangers.

- *The Christmas of Childhood*
  when we understand the roots of our
  Christmas expectations and reactions.

- *The Christmas of Selfhood*
  when we find the renewal of who we
  are and who we intend to become in the
  new year.

Each Christmas experience and celebration
offers unique activity, meaning and blessing.
Each brings a transcendence of meaning to our
souls. Each is actually a frontier of new awareness. What joy these Christmases offer you!

As you consider and contemplate, you will find the recognition of and reflection on these six distinctions of Christmas experiences and celebrations liberating and illuminating. The distinctions will provide more clarity about the impact of Christmas in your soul. You will feel more freedom in how you celebrate, respond and evolve or resolve each Christmas experience. Last, you will finally know how to creatively and consciously use the forces of Christmas to nurture your soul and determine the path of your life's next year. You will come to cosmically, socially and personally celebrate yourself (and everyone else) as:

A Being of Nature

A Being of Divine Origin and Purpose

A Being of Material Existence and Creativity

A Being of Community

A Being of Unique Experiences and Stories

A Being of Evolving Individuality

This process continues and deepens. You discover newer and richer Christmas meaning as you celebrate Christmas in your soul each year.

ALL GLORY, LAUD AND HONOR

What is celebration? A celebration marks an occasion of pleasure. A celebration can also praise and acknowledge with glory, laud and honor. Celebrations divide into two extremes, the sensuous and the solemn. They can encourage lusty indulgences and wild behaviors or bring sobering and reverent gestures of restraint and quiet contemplation. We have our sacred and our profane celebrations.

Reflect on the celebrations of your life:

Birthday parties

Sunday Services

Birth celebrations: Baptism and Bris

Wedding and Baby Showers

Bachelor Parties

Weddings,

Funerals

4th of July Barbecues

High Holy Days

Fundraisers

Watching Award Shows

The Superbowl

　　　　　　　　　　　　Introduction

And so on...

Do you find pleasure in celebration?

Do you find comfort in celebration?

Do you find meaning in celebration?

Imagine creating a celebration of pleasure. Let go of all preconceptions and simply create a celebration of incredible pleasure. What is the occasion for celebration? What sensory delights are present? Who is celebrating with you or are you alone? Can you indulge your senses and feel the pleasure? Do you feel pleasure in pleasure?

Imagine creating a celebration of honor, laud and glory. Who or what is being celebrated? What are the symbols of celebration? What are the rituals of celebration? What are the stages of celebration? How do you feel working into the depths and up to the heights of this celebration? Are you excited or calmed? Do you feel a mood of honor? Are there loud fanfares or silence?

There are so many times in our lives that call out for celebration. Some are once-in-a-lifetime celebrations, but many return every year. How wonderful to know what you desire in the celebrations you create or participate in. We let tradition, family, capitalistic merchandising, religion or nationalism tell us what and how to celebrate. These "dictates" need to be enlivened with our own free will, our own choices regarding our celebrations.

Celebrations have many reasons and many ways to reach into the heights, depths and breadths of our earthly and spiritual realities. To celebrate most fully we must both marry and distinguish these two realities at this time of year. At Christmas, "celebration" acknowledges both the earthly and the spiritual as we participate in earthly revelry and spiritual revelation. As we intimately explore the six Christmas celebrations, we discover the hidden spiritual revelation in the earthly revelry and the essential reasons for earthly revelry living in the spiritual revelation. We learn that Christmas is, indeed, a many splendored celebration for our souls.

Celebration, whether sacred or sensuous, indicates the honoring and revering of an individual, the significance of an historical event and/or the spiritual or personal connection to a mood, a time of year, an individual, a deed, or an event. This definition asks us to recognize the cosmic, social and personal significances of the person, the mood, the holiday, the accomplishment or the event.

The three contexts and the six celebrations of Christmas provide meaningful and formative substance for the year. They give our souls the opportunity to address the totality of our being regardless of our religious beliefs and training. Celebration at Christmas time has occurred every year since the earth began encircling the Sun and the Sun began shining the light of life on the earth. We will continue to celebrate at Christmas time as long as we live.

The time has come for our souls to find the way to their own sense of Christmas, the cosmic, the social and the personal, free of any external cultural, religious or biographical dogmas or demands. Create your own celebration of Christmas. Create your own celebration of yourself.

CELEBRATING CHRISTMAS

The following pages bring descriptions, personal narrative and questions providing new understandings and insights about your personal relationship to Christmas. With awareness of the six distinct Christmas celebrations, you can ultimately create your very own Christmas celebration with clarity, free of confusion or conflict.

With attention, each of the six Christmas

celebrations begins to live independently. Every year you can choose which Christmases you want to celebrate to serve your inner path of self-development. Give yourself sacred permission to form and fulfill a free, creative relationship to all six Christmases.

Each Christmas offers many gifts to your soul. When you have read about each Christmas, ask yourself what you love about each Christmas. How does each Christmas bless your sense of self. Make a what-I-want-from-Christmas list for each of the six Christmases. These are Christmas gifts of new feelings, new experiences, new awareness. These are gifts for your senses and your soul. Make a list of what feelings and experiences you want to give to others for each Christmas—how you want to make each Christmas come alive for those you love. Record the gifts you have received from each Christmas—the gifts you wished for and the gifts that surprised you.

In the book I share my thoughts and perceptions of each Christmas experience. I look at the external realities of each Christmas and explore the archetypal and mystical image living in each reality. Then, I ask questions to awaken, not just personal memories, but personal meaning. I want you to realize the intimate significance each Christmas holds for your soul.

Read and relate to the descriptions of the six Christmases but also work with personal question: What does this Christmas mean to me? Study your relationship to each Christmas. Each brings joy and wisdom to your soul. Each, also, may bring a shadow or a challenge to your soul.

In contemplating Christmas, examine your thoughts and perceptions of each of the six Christmases, examine your feelings, positive, negative and neutral, about each aspect of Christmas and examine what you do, all that you do, in engaging with each Christmas.

Your life during the year will be enriched, comforted, empowered, even healed, by your attention to these distinct experiences of Christmas. As you deepen your celebration of each Christmas, you deepen your celebration of each part of your soul and the full expression of your humanity.

The Christmas
of Nature

The Christmas of Nature

Nature's Christmas celebrates the (re)birth of the sun. It reveres the yearly cycle of life and the power of the sun in shaping life's cycle. It offers reassurance that light will overtake darkness, warmth will overtake cold and life will return to the earth. This is the Christmas that has always been and always will be.

ANCIENT CHRISTMAS

Imagine living when the earth was young and pure. Imagine human consciousness 10,000 years ago. The soul of ancient consciousness read nature the way we now read books. Our senses attended exquisitely to the nuances of light, growth, movement and death.

We listened to the spiritual being, the god, behind every physical entity. Daffodils spoke. Great pines spoke. Rocks spoke. Streams spoke. These gods were experienced in nature, not the soul. Nature gods provided, protected and punished. These gods commanded the totality of existence and the meaning, of creation and destruction. And the human soul was humbled and awed.

What did it mean to experience nature grow silent as darkness deepened, cold increased, and the plants and animals dramatically changed appearance and activity? Imagine seeing the sky fill with birds taking away their songs and leaving silence behind as they fly after the sun. How did the ancient soul respond to seeing flowers and leaves fade and fall, turning the earth somber and barren? Everything in nature and daily existence diminished. The gods had abandoned. Life was lost.

Imagine not knowing, not being certain, that there would be a return.

Then one day the dark heavens with the moving stars and changing moon become still. At that moment the wise ones who read the stars began to tell stories of the sun god being reborn. They said that this birth would bring returning light, warmth and life. The gods would return.

The shaman tells his people they must dance and sing a new sun into birth. This ritual seems to last forever. For three nights the ritual goes on. The darkness seems to have conquered light.

Then on the third day the light grows stronger declaring a new sun god is born. The simple, innocent, ancient soul feels joy.

THE CYCLE OF THE SUN

Reaching into this primeval Christmas and its meaning to the soul experience of early human consciousness, reveals a clarifying foundation to our mysterious need for all Christmases. It is Christmas as the turning point from fear and doubt to hope and confidence. The sun that has been decreasing, losing the battle with darkness, begins to increase. With the increase comes the rebirth of nature, the source and harmonizer of all life. Nature's Christmas tells us life is cyclical and asks us to pay attention to the wisdom of life's cycles.

The impact of life as cycle is very hard for our modern soul to notice or feel. We have removed ourselves from the changing vulnerable world of nature and wrapped ourselves in the sameness and insulation of technology. We still sense the yearly fluctuations between the sun's presence and absence as we wake up to our clock radios and commute to and from work in the varying degrees of dawn and dusk, but we no longer concern ourselves with nature as life source and life harmonizer. Naively, or arrogantly, we no longer feel our lives dependent on the cycles of the sun.

Nor do we see or feel the sun as sacred cosmic mystery. The need and success of the human intellect to measure, quantify, explain and dominate all mysteries of earthly life has taken away many "unexplainable" experiences of the sun and of nature that once enriched the soul. We know the sun is not dying when our days grow shorter and shorter. We learn as young children that when it is dark in our part of the world, it is light in another. Except for our electric bill and the selling of sunscreen we pay little attention to the power of the sun. We take for granted its light, warmth and radiance. And in the dark of winter, we turn the thermostat up and light our gas fireplace or pack our bags and hop the cheapest flight to the warmth and light of islands.

Yet, each of us relates to the sun with every beat of our heart and with every breath we take. The sun moves through the entire zodiac, the twelve constellations every 25,920 years, called the Great Year. Our breathing pattern of each day reflects this solar movement. Each day, based on 18 breaths per minute, we take 25,920 breaths. For each breath our heart beats 4 times reflecting the four seasons of each year. The Cosmos, nature and the human are one and we celebrate, and embody this each year through the Christmas of Nature.

WITHOUT A CALENDAR

Nature's Christmas was and _is_ independent of the calendar. It does not depend on a date. The solstice was known and celebrated long before there was a need to measure and label time. The course of the seasons and the cycles of fertility measured time for early human consciousness. Nature's Christmas awakens in the part of our soul that carries our ancient archetypal memories. For thousands of years nature's Christmas was our only Christmas and the primary celebration of rebirth. The primeval soul was sensitive to the movement of the sun and the changing relationship between light and dark regardless of where on the planet the soul dwelled.

The Winter Solstice coincides with the other Christmases in the Northern Hemisphere. Rome, the seat of the early Christian Church, is located in this hemisphere. South of the Equator, Winter Solstice occurs in late June. The Christmases of Nativity, Riches, Relationships and Childhood are tied to our calendar consciousness and are celebrated on December 25 for the entire planet. The Christmas of Selfhood is connected to both the sun and the calendar—it lives in the calendar of the soul.

Nature and the Soul's Imagination

Wherever you live, and many of us have lived in many different places, the celebration of the Christmas of Nature is shaped by location and the sun's light.

My first seven Christmases were dark and cold in the mid-Atlantic nature of Long Island. Snow and sleigh bells were always a real possibility.

Then, as a troubled, vulnerable girl of eight, I had my first warm Christmas in Deerfield Beach, Florida. It was also my first Christmas without my father as my mother had divorced him and moved us to South Florida. I could not depend on the natural landscape, the temperatures or the lifestyle to guide my Christmas experience. Toys were the joys of my Christmas, but the dramatic change in my natural surroundings struck my heart with strangeness. I missed my nature's Christmas of cold silence as I went swimming, instead of sledding!

Now I live in an urban environment and there are no flowers and trees around me, just cement, steel and glass. Electric lights in buildings and on the street take away the starry mysteries of the night. Pigeons waddle on the sidewalks and rarely take flight. All the four-legged animals I see are on a leash. Snow may fall in the countryside, but less and less falls where I live. I miss the signs and silence of winter. Yet the Christmas of Nature lives vividly in my imagination and in my soul's experience.

While my senses experience the Christmas of the meteorologists, my cultural life offers the white Christmas environment as portrayed by Hollywood and Hallmark. Neither the weathermen nor the media moguls provide me with a true sense of nature at Christmas time. What does my soul seek? What is the inner meaning of the Christmas of Nature to me?

It doesn't matter if you are in the Southern Hemisphere or the Northern Hemisphere, near the equator or close to the poles—what matters is how alive your spiritual imagination is. Your earthly environment, your relationship to the sun, may align with your imagination or not. Your soul may connect deeply to the sense perceptible seasonal realities or not. For the Inner Year only the seasons of your soul determine your festivals and moods.

A Note To the Southern Hemisphere

Readers living in the Southern Hemisphere, your natural world meets the Sun in the reverse relationship of my Northern Temperate experience. Your Nature's Christmas comes at a far different time of year from the other Christmases. Does this alter the experience or the meaning of the Christmas of Nature? That's up to you and is dependent upon the balance between your soul's inner imagination and your outer perceptions.

The individuals who determined the dates of the Christian festivals lived in the Northern Hemisphere long before there was awareness that the Earth was a globe. They made their dating decisions based on the Gospels and the seasonal Pagan Festivals (which in so many ways reflected the unfolding significance of the events of the story of Jesus). The Nativity of Jesus has no date reference in the Bible, so the Christian Church fathers, through much controversy, chose the time of the winter solstice.

Although there was much debate and disagreement over the exact date on which to celebrate the Christmas of Nativity, the significance of the birth of the Son of God and the significance of the (re)birth of the sun have a

The Christmas of Nature

cosmic affinity. As sacred gestures of both the human and the divine (the natural and the supersensible) both Christmases fit together in the soul's cosmic imagination. Therefore, those in the Southern Hemisphere are asked to pay deeper attention to how and when their souls experience the Christmas of Nature.

If we pay unique attention to Nature's Christmas—not because of images on Christmas cards or the words of carols and songs, but because deep in each cell of our bodies we feel a "rebirth" of light and warmth in our bodies and souls. This rebirth of our "inner" sun greets the rebirth of the "outer" sun. In celebrating an *Inner Christmas* of nature we briefly still the movement of our souls in anticipation of our inner light rebirth. We have an Inner Solstice synchronizing with the Winter Solstice.

How aware are we of the Winter Solstice? In our modern times, we can listen to the news or read the paper and learn the exact time of Winter Solstice. Our intellects love this curious scientific fact but our souls deep in their primordial needs, feel a subtle, but deep, longing. We desire the *mystery* of the Great Cycle of Death and Rebirth of Light. The Christmas of Nature has been eclipsed by technology. We need to remember and feel the cosmic meaning of the solstice in our souls.

How Do You Experience Nature's Christmas?

How do you experience the seasons of the year? How sensitive are you to the transitions between the seasons? Do you respond just to your perceptions of light, temperature and the flow of life or do you also have a sense of the seasons in your soul?

If you have lived in different places, how did you experience the difference in the light? The flora and fauna? The mood of your fellow inhabitants?

Do you enjoy seasonal celebrations—religious, cultural, and national holidays? Are you aware that though these days have historical significance, they are rooted in the movement of the sun and the natural activity of the year?

What are your emotions around flowers and trees? Do you look for early green shoots? Do you study the leaves, buds, blooms and fruits? What do you feel when you see the bright red leaves of the maple tree in October? How do you respond to the bare branches of late autumn? Have you ever thought about the seeds deep in the earth during winter?

Do you realize that the increasing winter sun warms the earth inviting seeds to germinate? Does the warmth of your will cause the germination of new ideas, new feelings and new intentions in your soul?

Do you pay any attention to the four turning points of the sun : Winter and Summer Solstices, Vernal and Autumnal Equinoxes? Do they feel sacred or scientific to you? Or both? Do you pay attention to the lunar cycle?

Do you like fires and candlelight? What about the other elements of earth, water and air? Do you prefer cold temperatures or warm ones? Is your thinking cool or warm?

Do you look at the stars on winter nights? Do they seem magical? How do you respond to the vastness of the celestial Cosmos? Do you feel that you matter and that you are a significant part of all that is?

Do you relate the seasons to your emotions? Which season saddens? Angers? Frightens? Or delights? Which season leads you to move toward your inner life with deep contemplation?

Which season leads you out of yourself into social or practical activities?

What response do you have to light and darkness? Where does your soul feel most at home—in light? In darkness?

Have you ever been scared of the dark? Why? What dangers or evil did you anticipate? Did light mean the restoration of safety and goodness?

Does Christmas make you think of nature? Do you relate wreaths, pine boughs and Christmas trees to nature ? Do you bring the ever(lasting)green, the symbol of eternal life, into your home as a sacred symbol rather than as a holiday decoration?

What do you love in nature? How do you love Nature? Why do you love nature? Remember you are a being of Nature celebrating the Christmas of Nature and celebrating nature in you.

The Christmas of Nature

The *Christmas* of *Nativity*

The Christmas of Nativity

The Christmas of Nativity celebrates the birth of Jesus. The story of this birth is told in the Luke and Matthew Gospels. This birth carries many levels of meaning to many souls. As with all the other Christmases, the deeper we go into the levels of meaning, the richer our celebrations become.

The Christmas of Nativity is celebrated with church services, particularly Midnight Services on Christmas Eve. In the dark of night people gather to find light and warmth. The lighting of candles, the singing of hymns and carols, the presence of the crèche or model of the Nativity scene, the ringing of bells and the reading of the Nativity story take place in Christian churches on Christmas Eve and again on Christmas morning all over the globe.

The Christmas of Nativity is a sacred ritual of great beauty and miraculous story. Many who never go to church at any other time of year and many who are not from a Christian heritage, love this religious Christmas because of its beauty, story and brevity. It is a joyful and hopeful moment in the long year.

Let's look at what we find living in this religious celebration that goes beyond the constraints of religious and sectarian doctrine and practice. All human souls can relate to the story of the Nativity once it is freed from organized Christianity. This freedom does not deny the beliefs and devotion of Christians. Rather the universal understanding brings home to every soul, the depth of comfort and meaning in both the sacred and human aspects of Nativity.

Unto Us A Child Is Born

When we find the spirit of the Christmas of Nativity we escape the coldness and grandiosity of our modern technological existence and enter into a humble mood of innocence and love. On Christmas Day the world stops and a newborn infant becomes the God of infinite compassion and eternal redemption. We feel the sins and the weight of the world fade. Peace comes to earth and goodwill blesses all because of the innocence and significance of a birth.

The Child's parents are not symbols of power and wealth. Poor and humble, they suffer adversity and indignity and must dwell in a stable with the animals for the birth of the Babe. The mother is full of grace. Her husband is strong and devoted. They surround the child with love and awe. The graceful devotion of the parents, the gentle simplicity of the stable, and the radiant innocence of the infant offer the longed for, but rarely known, feeling of family intimacy and reverent nurturance.

The Child sleeps calmly, protected by angels and animals, and revered by simple shepherds and wise kings alike. Could we imagine ourselves so protected and revered?

Our hearts find such comfort with this nativity scene. We want to believe, if only for a few minutes in the year, that innocence heals suffering, that hope redeems despair, and that death is overcome by eternal life—all because a child is born.

Joy To The World

Christmas Eve services bring together families and community. We join together for a joyful celebration of all that is good in the story of the Nativity. The Babe was born for everyone's benefit, blessing and redemption, and during the service all voices sing the reassuring, comforting and familiar carols—the promises of peace and joy have renewed possibility for our souls and the world. For many of us, Christmas Eve is the only religious service we traditionally attend during the entire year and, for many more of us who don't go to Midnight Mass, we think about the service and the birth it celebrates.

There is a primal need in the human soul for a ritual that acknowledges mystery and miracle. The Christmas of Nativity, with it's comforting and intimate gesture, reaches into those forgotten longings and pulls at them, like a flickering candle flame in a dark cave.

Religion comes from the Latin root *re-ligio*—to reunite. A cosmic religious gesture exists in the Christmas of Nativity that reunites us with our families, with our friends, with our innocent desires for goodwill and with our sense, however conscious, of the spiritual living in our souls. The Christmas of Nativity does not require that we feel sadness, guilt or remorse. We are asked to feel like little children—happy, loved and blessed by a newborn king. What other religious festival asks so little and gives so much?

A Heart to Hear Angels Sing and A Head To Follow The Star

The Christmas of Nativity asks us to hear angels singing of glory and peace and to follow a star to a manger holding the infant King of Kings.

To hear the song of angels we must have the heart of a simple shepherd. In our modern lives, identifying with the image of a shepherd resting on the warm earth in the deep of night awakening to the music of a host of angels is not easy. No, the heavenly host does not come in an MP3 file on your iPod but we still have our listening hearts. Our hearts remain simple in spite of our materialistic sophistication. Our hearts can look up to the cosmic stars and hear the hosts of angels.

To read the cosmic wisdom of a star requires a different head than the ones that designed the Hubble Spacecraft. What kind of believing eyes can follow a star and what kind of intelligence seeks the knowledge within great mysteries? Could you find the wisdom in your thinking to recognize and respond to the hidden language of the stars?

Christmas Eve services attract us because in our deepest soul we want to know the mood and the images that live behind the carols and the scriptures of the Nativity. Can we imagine having a heart and a head sensitive to the innocence and the wisdom of the Holiest Night of the year?

I repeat, we must be like the humblest of shepherds to hear the angels sing of the goodness in our souls and the wisest of kings to follow the Star to the new beginning of our inner lives.

Both the shepherds and the kings are willing to travel. Is your soul willing to travel? Where in the vast realms of your soul, is your destination? Do you seek a manger in your own soul? Is there something born in your soul during Christmas you long to revere? Listen to your inner angelic hosts—they are in the place of your soul where you guard your sheep. Find your star shining in the dark night of your soul life.

One of the blessings of traveling to the manger of your soul during *Inner Christmas*, is the awakening of both the shepherd and king within your soul. You reconnect with the earth and the heavens of your being. You become gentler in your feeling heart and sounder in your thinking head.

SHARING THE LIGHT

Our Christmas of Nativity is shared with others in the churches of our local communities. More and more churches are paying attention to the social aspects of religion. I love the ceremony, or ritual, of lighting candles. In the darkened sanctuary everyone holds an unlit candle. No one has a flame. Then a lit candle appears, not to shine in solitude but to pass the flame on to one of the unlit candles. Each candle receives its flame from another candle and lights the flame of the next candle. The growing light—such a warm glow—illuminates the church community. The light grows because each member of the community is willing to light another member's candle. We create and celebrate sharing light in the dark of Christmas Eve.

The Christmas of Nativity is about belief, ritual and story. It is about divine birth, earthly simplicity, celestial glory, and faithful devotion. It brings together, kings and shepherds, animals and gods, a mother and child. So much more than mere dogma will resonate in our souls if we bring a searching openness to all that lives in the Christmas of Nativity.

Put in a CD of the Messiah or the Vienna

Boys Choir singing the great Christmas Carols, and spend some quiet time thinking about your experience of the Christmas of Nativity. You may find some surprising and insightful gifts appearing in your soul. You will find yourself stepping over the threshold between unconscious tradition and dogma to a conscious and free experience of divine mystery.

HOW DO YOU EXPERIENCE THE CHRISTMAS OF NATIVITY?

What do you love about the Christmas of Nativity? Do you love the story of the Nativity? Do you believe it? What are your questions about the Nativity Story?

How do you celebrate the Christmas of Nativity? Do you go to church during the Christmas season? Are church services the only way to celebrate the Christmas of Nativity? Do you bring out a creche each year? How would you enrich this experience?

Is it important to share the Christmas of Nativity with your family and friends or do you feel fulfilled celebrating it in a solitary way?

Write a Christmas Prayer of Love from your Christmas heart. Each of us has the spiritual creativity to write a prayer or a meditative verse. Just begin and let the words flow. Write one prayer about the Holy Family and the journey to the manger. Write another one about the warm simplicity of the shepherds and the angelic Hosts. Write a third prayer about the wisdom of the three Kings and their willingness to follow a star. Write a fourth one to the Infant Jesus and to your own innocent divinity.

Writing prayers reconnects us with our own direct link to the Divine. The prayers of others may be comforting and inspiring, but the experience of writing your own prayer is transcendent and awakening.

The Christmas
of Riches

The Christmas of Riches

The Christmas of Riches is everyone's Christmas. Even if you have no Christmas of Childhood to remember, no belief in the Christmas of Nativity, no awareness of the Christmas of Nature, and no family for the Christmas of Relationships, you will experience the Christmas of Riches. You can't avoid it. From November to January, it's everywhere.

With its roots in the transformative rites of nature and religion and its focus on the senses and the material, the Christmas of Riches provides an irresistible gift to our lives. At Christmas time we find a collective and extravagant explosion of sensuous beauty and pleasure. In the deep darkness of the year, our surroundings burst with colorful fantasy, altering our sense of daily reality and rescuing us from the ordinary and the routine. Feasts, parties, and gifts warm our social interactions and create a loving sparkle in our eyes and a gentle ring to our voices.

The Christmas of Riches is the Christmas we see, taste, smell and hear. It is a festival of earthly delights and pleasures. We celebrate what we can possess and enjoy with our senses. Human beings love to indulge. Christmas is the time of the year when indulgence explodes in our lives. There is no collective restraint as we all shout "MORE!" We seem to never have enough of Christmas' sensuous delights.

Christmas, the most visual of our holidays, alters the appearance of our spaces. Through Christmas adornment, decorations and "surgical" transformation we seek the immortality, perfection and creativity of the gods. We establish both earthly and heavenly paradise and beauty. Ideally, we celebrate a ritual of conscious reverence as we create the symbolic and beautiful images of the holiday.

As you look at the visual delights of the Christmas of Riches, consider how you experience indulgence and adornment in your soul. Consider what each aspect of adornment and decoration means to you?

What follows are a few imaginations to help you experience the meanings living in all the elements of the Christmas of Riches.

DECK THE HALLS

Every Christmas, we decorate madly and magically. We transform our private spaces and our public spaces into winter wonderlands. Lustrous colors appear in decorations of every shape and size. Lights are strung everywhere bringing heavenly skies down to front yards, living rooms and the biggest evergreen in town. At home, we begin at the lamppost move to the front door and into the living room. In some homes every room is richly decorated. Our homes, our stores, our offices and our streets become glittery jewels and overflowing cornucopias.

Every Christmas, we visually declare ourselves "royalty" living in a fairyland. Abundance is the mode. I have a friend who has no children but fills her living room each year with over 100 Santas of every shape and size. Christmas is not ordinary, nor is it a time of scarcity. We make our spaces altars to the sugarplum fairy and the god of plenty.

Our holiday decorating styles were first defined in the opulent palaces of Queen Victoria. The very popular Queen Victoria and her beloved Prince Albert shared great love and great influence. Albert was a German prince

The Christmas of Riches

and Victoria wanted him to feel at home in her English palaces, so she embraced the German tradition of an indoor tree at Christmas. In 1846, the London News published a drawing of the royal family standing around a decorated tree. Immediately, the public imitated the scene in their parlors and drawing rooms. Fascinated with English royalty, Americans quickly followed. It is with Victorian royal blessing that the German Christmas tree reigns as the decorative center of the season.

Since Victoria and Albert's mid-nineteenth century influence, many families and many communities begin the Christmas holidays around the tree. Joining the tree are the wreath, the boughs, the fruit, all symbols of everlasting, ever abundant gifts of Mother Nature.

The Tree Decorations

A trip to the attic or the top of a closet brings down the myriad decorative goodies. Each box is filled with personal treasures. We open them up and our hearts fill with memories and excitement. With a sense of personal ritual we hang each ornament, finding just the right branch on which to place a small bit of luxury, whimsy or memory. There is something very meaningful in the fact that the ornaments are fragile, easily broken, and hang from thin wires. This delicacy of the ornaments seems to reflect the overall mood of the holiday: that it is precious and transient—in a few days it will all disappear back to the boxes in the attic or top of the closet.

Many find joy and comfort in decorating their tree and their home in the same way year after year. Maybe a few new ornaments will be added each year but essentially the Christmas Tree is the never-changing fixture of Christmas. The same angel or star is on the top of the tree. A friend speaks with great nostalgia of his childhood living room with the tree and the incredible electric trains covering the floor. Ritual and sameness are very soothing in our modern world of endless change and updating.

Others like to find a new theme for their Christmas decorations every year. Creating new decorative themes requires so much imagination and so much money. How many ways can you create a Christmas fantasy? Twice I have decorated a Christmas tree in a special way. When I was in my early twenties I had gone to the Georgia coast right before Christmas and found the beach filled with sand dollars of all sizes. I gathered about thirty in various sizes and brought them home to my tiny apartment. After bleaching them to a pristine whiteness, I hung the sand dollars on my tiny tree with red and green satin ribbons. It was so beautiful. Years later I decorated a very tall tree with balls of many colors and sizes. Uniquely, I began at the top with all the gold ornaments, then with silver, yellow, pink, red, green, blue and purple. I spiraled the colors down the tree from the gold of the sun to the deep purple of the earth. My kids called my creation the "Rainbow Tree". Sadly, we had a little kitten who loved the tree and the ornaments. She climbed the tree at every chance and in response to her movements most of the balls of the rainbow fell crashing to the earth.

We decorate our trees with symbols. The most classic decoration is the ball. These iridescent spheres of color symbolize unity, the world, the sun, and the soul. There is a meaning beyond, behind, and above the physical globe. Does that make a difference to you? What are the meanings behind your Christmas ornaments? We decorate our tree with symbols of the Christmas past, with the six-sided shapes of snowflakes, with miniatures of musical instruments, with angels and so on. I have seen ornaments in the shape of pickles—kosher, of course. When we decorate with objects of beauty, sentiment or humor, we are saying something. Yes, we can keep it all superficial, but how sad to overlook the manifold and glorious, cosmic and intimate meanings living in our decorations. On the branches of the tree that represents everlasting life and points to the heavens, what meanings do you want to hang?

If you, your family and friends love your Christmas trees, just for their visual delight or the wonderful flow of tradition and memory from one year to the next, how perfect. If your desires for the Christmas of Riches are beginning to seek more consciousness and meaning but you don't want to abandon your familiar tree of sensory and sentimental delight, have a second tree. Place a small tree of Christmas Meaning on a table and cover it with the symbols of your life. Or have three trees, a tree of Christmas Past, a tree of Christmas Present and a tree of Christmas Future. Or a celestial tree, an animal tree, and a relationship tree. If you don't want to have a living tree, do your tree(s) of meaning as a drawing or a collage each year. You can bring this imagination of special meaning trees to your families. Build an imagination of what kind of Christmas tree each member would like. Don't be afraid of being humorous and don't be afraid of being profound.

THE WREATH

From the sphere of the ornamental Christmas balls, we move to the circle of the wreath on our doors with its image of the cycle of the year, of life, of friendship. The wreath welcomes all our visitors into our circle of love.

Wreaths are made of plant materials. Every plant connects to a soul meaning. If we research the meaning of the plants that form our wreath, we will discover that what appeals to our eyes is also appealing to our souls.

Often we put a bow on a wreath. Perhaps the bow symbolizes how we are all tied together in our journey through the cycles of our years. This circle of love is a great gift to each of us.

The wreath is among the many Christmas decorations that Nature gives us. We find much decorative natural beauty, beginning with the tree. We use dried flowers, berries, and greens. We string popcorn and cranberries. We decorate with fruits ripe with sweetness symbolizing our wish for the sweet nurturing substance of a happy, loving soul.

CHRISTMAS LIGHTS

Every Christmas, we turn the earthly into the heavenly. We bring the stars from the sky down to every Main Street and into every living room. From a single simple candle to endless strings of electric lights flashing to music, the Christmas of Riches sparkles.

It is said that Martin Luther was walking in a forest one Christmas night. When he got home to his family he took every candle in the house and placed them on the branches of their tree. He wanted to share the experience of seeing the stars twinkling through the evergreens. If true, we must be grateful to his inspiration. We can't fly among the stars but we can bring the stars down to us, and live among them a few weeks every year.

The lights of Christmas include the light and warmth of flames whether from the single flame of a candle or from the crackling fire in the hearth. Being toasty by the fire or glowing with reflections of candlelight melts the cold winter's frost with Christmas warmth. Like the burning Yule log in ancient pagan solstice celebrations, the light and warmth of fires at Christmas assure us that we are safe, protected and blessed.

Can you describe what lights ups in your soul at Christmas? Do these lights sparkle and shine through the rest of the year or do they dim and darken quickly?

Christmas Colors

Christmas without color would not be Christmas. Our eyes feast on colors with a sensitivity that is not present the rest of the year. Each color reflects a part of the magic of the season.

The classical pairs of Christmas colors, red and green and silver and gold, are opposites, symbolizing the worldly and the spiritual. Green, the color of the leaf, and red, the color of bloom and berry are earthly colors. The celestial colors are silver for moonlight and the night, and gold for sunlight and the day. Red and white are also classical Christmas colors bringing the symbolic polarities of our souls. Red represents wisdom and white, innocence.

Red and green are opposites on the color wheel. They create a visual experience of balance and completeness. Red and green provide a deep unconscious perception that Christmas brings harmony and helps us maintain an inner feeling of peace on earth, goodwill to humankind. How do you find balance at Christmas?

Rainbows are present during Christmas providing all the colors of light to illuminate the Christmas of Riches. The rainbow symbolizes the essential diversity and reflective harmony of the cosmos, of nature and of humanity. Our personalities appearing in our unique thoughts and our expressive actions have the richness of the rainbow and offer us the many soul gifts of Christmas.

How do colors affect you at Christmas? Do you have favorite Christmas colors? Can you imagine a Christmas that was just earthly in its colors or just celestial? How would each feel with out the balance of the opposite? If you prefer earthly to the celestial, what does it tell you about your personality, or how you relate to practical matters and spiritual matters?

THE FOODS AND FLAVORS

The Christmas of Riches celebrates the trinity of decorations, gifts and feasts. Most of us want plenty of these three elements of Christmas. Though circumstances may force us to scrimp in some way on decorations and gifts, we never hold back on the feasting. "Feast" is defined as a significant meal and as "something that gives us a great deal of pleasure." Whoever wrote that definition was thinking of our Christmas meals and all the holiday goodies.

Many of us have at least three Christmas feasts: Christmas Eve dinner, Christmas breakfast or brunch, and Christmas dinner. Each meal comes with traditional foods and special treats. It is not just our tummies that love this time of year; our hearts fill with love as we prepare the feasts. With Christmas feasts we are doing something special, sensuous and social. There is a real quality of love that goes into our Christmas meal-making and even the cleaning-up on December 24th and 25th.

Christmas foods taste good, smell good, look good and are shared with those we love. The meat, poultry and fish are always plump and juicy. The vegetables and salads are colorful and flavorful. The sweets are rich, gooey and dense. These foods are part of the intense sensory pageantry of our holidays, and the memory (and anticipation) of sharing them with others fills us with joy.

Christmas is the sweetest of holidays. Many who spend the year avoiding desserts, indulge in yummy confections during this season of sugar. Christmas treats are not simple desserts and sweets. They are elaborate, colorful and beautiful. We become architects of Gingerbread Houses, sculpt amazing figures with marzipan, and outdo nature with chocolaty Yule logs with meringue mushrooms. Moreover, the annual tradition of making dozens and dozens of Christmas cookies, fruitcakes or stollen to give to family and friends creates smiles of sugar on most faces, young and old. This holiday indulgence is not surprising. Sweet tastes tell the soul "all is well." And make us feel like we live in a sugary cocoon of Christmas joy.

GOOD CHEER

The desire to be of "good cheer" makes the Christmas of Riches a drinking Christmas as we wish each other well and toast to our riches with family and friends. Even those who completely disregard the religious elements of Christmas, turn to the "spirits" with eagerness, as alcohol is conducive of the expansive and generous mood of the season. No other holiday has so many special drinks: eggnog, grog, wassail, champagne, mulled wine, hot buttered rum, etc. And these are just the traditional drinks, more are created by clever bartenders every year. "Wassail" means "Good health be with you" and it is one of the traditional drinks that, although you may not know what it is made from or ever tasted it, you know it means Christmas cheer. Although rarely a gift on other holidays, giving bottled "spirits" is popular at Christmas.

To ward off the "chill" of winter, we share the social warmth and the "buzz" that comes from alcohol during the holiday. Our soul wants to lift itself up to the spirit of life and the spirit of the heavens as we drink to the good health and wealth of Christmas.

CHRISTMAS SMELLS

The smells of the Christmas of Riches come from three sources, Nature, the kitchen, and fire. The sense of smell arouses intimacy and evokes memories. Intimacy and memory are two of the sweetest joys of Christmas. Can you imagine Christmas without the following smells?

During Christmas, Nature comes into the house and gives us the deep awakening whiffs of evergreens. The Christmas smells of the plant world are not from the short-lived flowers, but from the needles, barks and leaves—the *ever*green or *ever*lasting members of the plant world. These smells prick us with liveliness. The smell of a freshly cut Christmas tree brings a mood of vibrancy to the "dead" of winter.

Many delicious smells come from the kitchen. These start our juices flowing in anticipation of the favorite tastes we will soon enjoy. The hearty aromas of roasting meat fill our homes for hours. But most of us focus on the sweet and spicy smells of Christmas. Cinnamon, allspice, nutmeg and cloves offer warming smells that remind our souls of the warmth of life. The sweetness of melting sugar reminds us that at Christmas our troubles "melt" away.

Last, Christmas provides the smells that emit from fire and flames reassuring us of the warmth of our homes and hearts. Chestnuts roasting on the open fire give us an earthy, grounding warmth, while scented candles delicately lead us upward like wisps of smoke into more ethereal realms.

SOUNDS

Everyone sings at Christmas. Most of us know the lyrics and tunes of Christmas music and feel enthusiastic about singing them with others. Whether we sound like a frog or an angel, we find ourselves singing at Christmas. When our voices join together in Christmas song our souls feel a communion, a shared goodness. Christmas songs close the musical gap between the generations. When else does that happen? Even a few rounds of "Jingle Bells" can bring the feeling that together we can laugh all the way through the coming year. This is the holiday of bells ringing and voices caroling.

How do you respond to the majesty of Handel's Messiah or the sentiment of "White Christmas?" Christmas music exalts our souls and our senses reflecting on the cosmic glory of the Nativity, the meaning of our relationships and the comfort of our homes in both the melodies and lyrics.

How does Christmas resound in your soul? Why do you have certain favorite carols and songs. Is it just sentimentality or is there a mood in the music or a significance in the words that enthralls your soul with Christmas meaning?

GIFTS

In the Christmas of Nativity, the gifts of the shepherds and kings are essential to the story. The gifts are tribute, a recognition. The simple gifts of the shepherds and the precious and rare gifts of the kings nurture, sustain and protect the Child.

Gifts at Christmas are very special gifts when they acknowledge what lives uniquely in the receiver. Imagine the gift-giving of Christmas as fitting tribute or as loving nurturance we offer to one another. When you make your Christmas gift list consider both gestures.

There are two other considerations with Christmas gifts: quantity and quality. What do you desire at Christmas, quantity or quality? How do your feelings about wanting the *most* or wanting the *best* shape your response, your satisfaction with Christmas?

Like inhaling and exhaling of life-bearing breath, the Christmas of Riches meaningfully exists in the gestures of giving and receiving. As the holiday nears we begin to think about *two* lists:

what we want to give, and

what we want to receive.

We contemplate both gestures equally. Contrary to the old adage, "It is better to give than to receive," it is truly as blessed to receive as it is to give and the "blessing" is the balance between the two. For every exhale, we inhale. The balance is not the measure of numbers or cost of the gifts but in the grace and thoughtfulness in our hearts as we receive and as we give.

Gifts must be chosen, made or purchased, and wrapped. We spend money, time and attention on the gifts we give. These days most of us have little of all three. Of money, time and attention, which makes the best gifts? This is a liberating question to consider. Who are the people in your life that you generously spend your attention on? Are they different people from the ones you chose to spend more money or more time on?

THE ECONOMY OF
THE CHRISTMAS OF RICHES

The Christmas of Riches has its own economy or management of resources. The resources of Christmas are interest, imagination, money, time and energy. Ask yourself if you have enough of these resources to support your Christmas of Riches. Is your Christmas economy thoughtful and wise? Does it reflect your reality or your fantasies?

The Christmas of Riches is an expensive Christmas as it requires a great deal of resources. Creating and enjoying all the riches costs much in energy, time and money. We need to have great amounts of interest and imagination. The riches can deplete and exhaust our resources. For some it is too much—too much to do and too much to experience.

Some individuals find the Christmas of Riches too rich for digestion—emotional, sensual, or spiritual digestion. Through digestion we take what exists outside of us and we make it our own being of body, soul and spirit. If you find the Christmas of Riches too much, you can evaluate and edit your traditions (see the appendix). Remake the Christmas of Riches into the Christmas of Enrichment. Enrich your body. Enrich your soul. Enrich your spirit.

Riches don't necessarily enrich. Perhaps Christmas *Less* is Christmas *More* for you. What do you want for your Christmas of Riches? What decorations? Foods? Music? Colors? Gifts and givings?

Some people have high sensitivity to sights, sounds, smells, textures or tastes. They are overstimulated, stressed out, energetically overloaded by the increase in sensory perception during the holidays. Some even call it sensory bombardment. If you have this high sensitivity, you are not crazy or bad. Nothing is weird about your negative feelings about this Christmas. There may well be neurological reasons for these feelings. There are many books for highly sensitive individuals that offer insight and healing.

You can be the designer and the editor of your Christmas riches. You can maximize what you love and minimize what you dislike. It is tough to alter the image you hold about Christmas. Many people want a "Queen Victoria" or "Martha Stewart" Christmas without the physical and emotional drain, but these Christmases are hardly possible without the wealth to pay others to manufacture the image for you rather than creating it yourself.

Every year magazines, books and videos are filled with advice on how to increase your Christmas riches. Lately, in contrast, there are articles and books on how to simplify Christmas. In our environmentally conscious times, we will be encouraged to celebrate a "Green" Christmas, instead of a "White" Christmas.

Use all these media generated Christmas formulas to inspire and liberate your imagination, rather than to seduce your desires and your wallet. You don't need to fall prey to the seductions of the holiday.

Years ago I was struggling with an emotional challenge—a dark, shadowy romance. In reflecting on this love story, I realized it had three chapters—seduce, abuse, abandon. The Christmas of Riches can seduce you with great fantasies, abuse you with demands and difficulties, and then abandon you as the holiday ends leaving you depleted and unfulfilled. Then the Christmas seductions begin all over again with heightened fantasies about next Christmas when you are certain you will have more time, more energy, more money and more satisfaction. You get caught in a loop of desires and disappointments.

If you identify with this Christmas pattern, there are ways to free yourself. When you feel yourself being seduced by fantasies, learn to say "No." When you feel abused, ask for help and set limitations. When you feel abandoned, reconnect with the true experience of Christmas—love. Use the insights of the six Christmases to help you manage your Christmases.

It is up to you to figure out how to make the Christmas of Riches enriching and restorative. Make a fantasy/reality chart. What is your fantasy? How much real time? How much real money? How much real energy? How much real depletion and exhaustion? Ask yourself if the outcome is going to be worth the input. Create a Grown-up's Christmas, not a Child's Christmas.

The Christmas of Riches

How do You Experience the Christmas of Riches?

What do you enjoy about Christmas Riches?

Write down your secular and sensuous traditions.

Are there traditions you would like to <u>add</u> to your Christmas? <u>Delete</u> from your Christmas?

Do you have any religious guilt or concerns about your participation in this non-religious celebration?

Do you feel that even the Christmas of Riches is Christian—just for Christians?

Do you ever feel guilty for indulging at Christmas? Or do you long to indulge more?

Do you consciously budget for Christmas in all the ways you will have expenses and income?

Give some thoughts to the images of abundance around your Christmas. Is it in the number of presents? The amount of food? The number of friends and family you get together with? Do you have feelings or judgments of scarcity, not enough, or excess, too much? What would a just "right" Christmas of Riches be?

The
Christmas of
Relationships

The Christmas of Relationships

Christmas celebrates our relationships. It is the yearly "hug," the time we embrace, physically or metaphorically, all those we are connected with through blood, affection, history, proximity or work. The Christmas of Relationships reconnects us through thoughts, calls, cards, letters, and visits. We surround all our relationships with a huge imaginary Christmas wreath of love.

THE WREATH OF LOVE

"Merry Christmas" we call out to others, feeling our own hearts warm. Relationships make Christmas merry—even if the relationship is the fleeting exchange of the two-word seasonal greeting between strangers. We wish each other a "Merry Christmas!" and living in that wish is the hope that all your relationships will surround you, and others with, joy and peace.

The archetype of the Christmas of Relationships is the Christmas of receiving and giving unconditional love from and to all others—over-riding Christmas as a time for only the well-behaved, the believing and practicing Christians, and those sharing culturally similar traditions. In the ideal, peace on earth reigns for all humanity, each and every one of us.

THE PEACEFUL FAMILY

Most of us would love to find the Christmas of Relationships bringing peace to our families. However, Christmas brings out the best and the worst in families. Christmas with your family can be a very tough and painful time. We all long for, and have a right to, a loving, recognizing and supporting family, especially at Christmas. Not all of us have this familial bliss. Expectations and guilt, anticipation and disappointment, hope and endurance can run high during the Christmas of Relationships.

What can you do to bring peace to your family at Christmas?

Christmas is the time many of us forgive others, and are forgiven, for hurt of all sorts, real and imagined. We may only temporarily find this forgiveness living in our families, but in that time we find glimmers of peace. We seek peace with all those with whom we share our life, our history, or our future. Peace appears only in the presence of forgiveness. Can we open up our Christmas hearts and say: I forgive those who make my life difficult in any way. I seek forgiveness from all those whose life has been made difficult by my thoughts, words or deeds. It is forgiveness that announces the goodwill that is the precursor of peace on Earth.

GOODWILL TO ALL

The Christmas of Relationships holds the promise of the Christmas of Goodwill. Our will is good when it serves others, not merely ourselves. Our will to exist, to imagine, and to act is filled with the intention to do good for others. We strengthen our <u>resolve</u> to be better human beings. Nowhere in our lives does "better" offer more possibility than in our deeds in relationship to other human beings. We call our intentions New Year's Resolutions in our secular culture but they are actually Christmas Resolutions. These intentions state our resolve to reflect and express "Peace on Earth to human souls of Goodwill."

Create your resolutions differently this year. Make a <u>goodwill</u> list—all your resolutions to bring peace on Earth. This is not the list of your resolutions to lose weight, keep your house clean, climb Mount Kilimanjaro, or learn Chinese.

Begin with considering your resolutions in relationship to each of the Seven Virtues: *Patience, Purity, Restraint, Generosity, Persistence, Kindness and Humility.* Then consider your resolutions in relationship to the Seven Vices or Deadly Sins: *Wrath, Lust, Gluttony, Greed, Sloth, Envy and Pride.* How does your will—your resolve or your intent—express patience? How does your will avoid greed? Working with the virtues and the vices—seeking more virtue and less vice in your life—brings clarity to how you bring Peace on Earth, peace in your relationships and peace to your soul.

EVERYONE'S BIRTHDAY

The Christmas of Relationships is the universal Nativity, the day of birth. It is everyone's unofficial birthday.

My birthday is December 11, 1947. That is <u>my</u> birthday but I really grow older by the Christmases I celebrate. Every Christmas I look at my family and my friends and I realize we are all a year older. I don't feel that way about Halloween or 4th of July or Thanksgiving. Christmas is the birthday we all share.

Christmas declares, like the sun, we have all lived another year. We have experienced each of the four seasons and the many changes of our soul as it moved through the year. Christmas says we experience life as reoccurring cycles, not as a linear continuum. We age with each cycle from Christmas to Christmas.

The goodwill of Christmas means we see each year as a growing of our capacity to do goodwill and love truly. We can imagine celebrating experiencing being a year wiser, freer, kinder. With each Christmas we can celebrate so much more than becoming older.

SAYING HELLO, SAYING GOODBYE

The Christmas of Relationships also celebrates the beginning of the cycle of life and the end of the cycle of life. The Christmas gathering is often the time when we joyfully welcome newborn family members. We share a first Christmas with the new lover or spouse of a relative (or, unknowingly, the last Christmas before a separation.) And, sadly, Christmas is the often the last time we visit with a beloved elderly family member.

We don't always know we are giving a parent, a grandparent, an aunt or a dear friend a last hug, saying our last Christmas goodbye. We don't anticipate that a relationship will end through death, estrangement or divorce. When we feel the absence and loss during Christmas, our grief grows deeper. The memories of the last Noel are achingly poignant.

Recall your memories of the Christmas hellos and Christmas goodbyes? Cherish these memories. How do you include grief in your Christmas joy? How do you include Christmas joy in your grief?

CHRISTMAS GENERATIONS

The awareness of the hellos and goodbyes of Christmas draws attention to one of the sweet photo-ops of the holiday, the multiple generational portrait. I have a picture of me at age two with my mother, grandmother and great-grandmother—the Christmas of Four Generations. I love this picture of the maternal stream of my family.

My older cousin lives about thirty miles away. Our busy lives mean our best intentions to visit during the year get forgotten, but for many years my cousin, Emily, invited my family to join hers for Christmas Eve dinner. Our extended family Christmas Eves began before my kids were born and when hers were toddlers. Now my aunt is 90 and Emily has grandchildren so she celebrates her own Christmases of Four Generations. I always feel my cousin provides a Norman Rockwell Christmas for me. What a blessing. Because our families have grown, we no longer give presents, but the familial love is as Christmas perfect as ever.

Christmas also helps us with the personal transition from child to young adult to young parent to middle aged parent, grandparent and great-grandparent. My daughter now cooks Christmas dinner, not me! How we age and let go of certain Christmas roles and responsibilities in our family traditions is a fascinating and mysterious process.

Do you have Christmases of Generations? How do you move from being the youngest to being the middle or the oldest generation?

OPENING HEART AND HOME

The Christmas of Relationships reaches beyond family. The wonderful Christmas intimacy goes beyond family ties to ties of life. My first husband was in Alcoholics Anonymous. Before our kids were born, each Christmas Day I prepared a huge Christmas feast for our AA "family." It was an open house and open heart celebration. The connecting thread of sobriety and the twelve steps made these Christmases of Relationship very intimate.

Some of my most cherished and intimate Christmas memories recall the yearly efforts to put on the Christmas fair at my children's school. All the parents and teachers worked for weeks to bring a warm and wonderful experience to our larger community. We prepared, we made it happen and we cleaned up. It was very hard work and a yearly Christmas of Relationships joy.

Have you ever created a Christmas Party for those who walk with you on a special path? Have you worked with a community of friends to create a Christmas event?

THE ANNUAL OFFICE PARTY

What does Christmas bring to your relationships at work? Christmas is the time of year when work relationships are feted. It is not the fiscal year that brings out food, drinks and music for the management and the staff, it's the Christmas of Relationships. The entire mood of the workplace changes at Christmas as people soften and engage with a different energy.

What is your mood at your annual Christmas party at your place of work? How do you feel about your boss or your subordinates when the spirit of Christmas embraces you?

Businesses use Christmas cards and gifts to build business relationships and to thank customers for doing business with them. This is relationship marketing because we all equate Christmas with good relationships.

Do you appreciate your business relationships at Christmas?

CHRISTMAS CHARITY

Finally, Christmas is the time we feel related to those who suffer. It is the time of Christmas charity. Perhaps you send money to your newspaper's "Neediest Families" fund, volunteer at a soup kitchen for Christmas Dinner, or make a generous donation to a favorite charity. The Christmas of Relationships inspires us to relate to people we will never meet but whose lives we may change.

How do express your generous heart at Christmas. Do you reach out to those in need during the holidays with your thoughts and prayers? Your time? Your money?

THE MELTING WARMTH OF CHRISTMAS

At Christmas our hearts reach out to strangers. We say hello with a special feeling and Merry Christmas with a heartfelt smile. As a greeting or a farewell, "Merry Christmas!" carries more authentic feeling than the greetings and farewells of other times of year. We are "wishing" something good and joyful to others. The mood of goodwill is powerful.

Of course, you may find a soul here and there who connects more to the "Bah Humbug!" gesture, but that is usually a sign of loneliness, bitterness and hurt. Give them a big Christmas smile and their aching hearts may find a little warming, healing comfort. Even the Scrooges of the world are part of our Christmas of Relationships.

THREE RELATIONSHIP IMAGINATIONS

To bring more awareness, rich with illuminating imagination, around your Christmas of Relationships, I suggest three imaginations. First, imagine a Christmas all by yourself. Second, imagine a Christmas shared with one special person. Finally, imagine a Christmas with twelve others. These should be revealing exercises. You will learn much about your feelings

The Christmas of Relationships

regarding yourself and others at this unique time of year. You will find you have more choice and more joy in celebrating you Christmas of Relationships.

A SOLITARY CHRISTMAS

Nobody wants to be alone on Christmas. We don't even want to think of a stranger being alone. Why?

Can we imagine a solitary Christmas? Why not? Let's explore an exercise in self-development by imagining a perfect, but solitary, Christmas.

It is Christmas morning and you wake up alone. Where are you? Are you at home or at some faraway place? What is the weather like? Do you have a Christmas Tree? What does it look like? Are there other decorations? Maybe you have no decorations! How does that feel? (Remember, you can create this solitary Christmas to be a perfect Christmas for your soul.) Do you eat special foods, drink special drinks? Any sweet indulgences? What about music? A walk? A bath or a nap?

Are the external and environmental elements insignificant? Do you want to focus on your inner life? What thoughts live in your solitary Christmas soul? Memories? Dreams? Do you read something? Write something?

What does this solitary Christmas feel like to you? Does it feel more spiritual or more sensual? Do you focus on memories of being with others or on the joys of being by yourself? Can you celebrate being alone on Christmas?

A CHRISTMAS OF ONE RELATIONSHIP

Now imagine a perfect Christmas of One Relationship. You are all alone in a comfortable place. There is a Christmas mood around you. There is a knock at the door. You open it and there stands someone you want to see. You invite him or her in. He or she has a gift for you. What is it? What gift do you have for her or him? What do you talk about? Do you tell this person how you feel about her or him? What you love and appreciate about who they are? What do you forgive? What do you apologize for? Just one person sharing a perfect Christmas with you.

The Christmas of Relationships

IMAGINE TWELVE CHRISTMAS VISITORS

You can imagine twelve different individuals coming one by one to visit you. They can be members of your family, friends, characters from a favorite novel, historical figures, holy saints, shepherds or kings, anyone, even Jesus or the Buddha. Each one brings you a gift and you have a gift for each one. Make the gifts ones of wisdom or wonder. Write down the gifts and write your feelings about the gifts—the ones received and the ones given. Have you prepared a special feast for these twelve visitors? When you say goodbye at the end of Christmas Day, what do you say to each of the twelve? What do they say to you? How do they interact with each other?

Working with twelve different individuals can be challenging, but twelve is the number of completion and perfection. Whatever twelve individuals you choose, as you imagine them surrounding and shaping your Christmas experience you will find many insights and surprises.

You can extend this exercise throughout the year—deepen your conversation with one individual a month. You might do this monthly exercise on the 25th of each month. The spirit of Christmas relationships will work within you each month with each Christmas partner. Remember to be open to your feeling impressions. You will find gifts of self-awareness coming with each month.

The
Christmas of
Childhood

The Christmas of Childhood

The Christmas of Childhood is the Christmas of vague and powerful memories that provide the emotional ground for all future Christmases. These memories are shaped during our first few Christmases. The Christmas of Childhood is personal. No one but you can reveal its particular meaning, not even your parents who shaped your early celebrations of Nature, Nativity, Riches and Relationships. Only you have the experiences and the memories.

I must warn you at this time: This chapter includes spoilers. It reveals a Christmas of Childhood that is far from a" Babes in Toyland" storybook. Most of us who are parents work hard to give our own children a storybook Christmas. Are we trying to give our children a Christmas we never had? Do we ever think about how this projected "storybook" Christmas impacts an innocent, unfolding soul?

What would be the ideal Christmas awakening for a growing child? How would we gently bring the experience of Christmas to a little one? How would we bring them into nature?

Would we tell stories and sing songs about the dark silence of the longest night?

How would we tell a child about the Nativity of a being of innocence, purity and compassion who would change the world and our souls?

Would we slowly bring small elements of the decorative symbols of Christmas into our homes creating a delicate magical transformation for their young senses to perceive without overwhelm? Would we choose their gifts, not for number and commercial dazzle, but for a sense of joy and creative awakening?

Would our family gatherings focus on warmth and serenity? Would we remind all our loving relatives and friends to refrain from baby talk and sugary treats and all that might over stimulate the babies and toddlers?

Imagine the depth of Christmas feeling a child would find in a gently unfolding holiday and how it would shape his/her inner life and emerging soul.

How might this approach to celebrating Christmas heal and affirm the Christmas longing in your adult soul?

However, several imagined Christmas needs conflict with or challenge this perspective of a gently unfolding Christmas experience for a child. What about the delights of Christmas excitement and intensity? Isn't Christmas the yearly time for indulgence and excess? (Historically, the days following the Winter Solstice were wild times.) Don't some children actually thrive on stimulation?

Let's be thoughtful and creative. And scientific! Our nervous system is most healthy when there is a harmonious balance between the excitatory and inhibitory neurotransmitters. When we are born we are mostly excitatory chemistry in order to have the energy to grab onto this new life. We develop our inhibitory chemistry as we mature and become self-harmonizing.

Our demanding times and our multi-tasking, high-powered daily lives are so stimulating that many of us, no matter what our age, turn to various activities and substances to calm ourselves down and to give ourselves a sense of a balanced inner nature. The pre-technological times that required "wild" celebrations were the opposite of ours—winter was so still and daily activity so routine and simple that the liveliness of the celebration brought much needed stimulation. But, do we need stimulation now?

The Christmas of Childhood

Christmas can be both calming and stimulating. To support the development of our inhibitory neurochemistry and a joyful sense of well-being, the Christmas of (Early) Childhood should focus on the calming and centering aspects of the holiday. Both parents and children will find a calm Christmas giving their souls gentle delight and sweet peace.

Our Christmases often strive to achieve the childhood dream of delight and avoid the childhood nightmare of disappointment and dysfunction. Revisiting our memories, the good and the bad, of the Christmas of Childhood can help free us from the anxieties of Christmas Past and allow us to enjoy Christmas Present. Let's consider the Christmas of Childhood by looking at the first four. Though these Christmases hold great impact, we probably have little memory of them.

OUR FIRST CHRISTMAS

Each of us has our first Christmas in the first year of our lives. We may be anywhere from minutes old to 364 days old.

I was two weeks old on my first Christmas. My daughter was 11 weeks old and my son was eight and a half months old—three very different stages of sensory and cognitive development with which to initially experience the many-layered impressions of Christmas.

Christmas changes everything. It's in the air. Our homes look different. The smells are different. The sounds are different. Christmas enhances, energizes, and even exaggerates our little worlds. Most importantly, Christmas changes our mother's mood.

The making of Christmas falls on our mothers. In face of new motherhood, or nurturing two or more children of different ages with different needs, Christmas comes along and expectations of perfection, long lists of to-dos, the struggles to be a good wife, a good daughter, a good friend, a good member of the community, cook a great feast, buy the best gifts and decorate the perfect house will stress any woman. A stressed mother stresses her young child. As little ones, even newborns, we instinctively experience our mother's stress level and mirror it. A gentle Christmas celebration is good for mother and child.

Often there are many more people around. People coo and smile and touch us with a kind of Christmas enthusiasm. We find ourselves in the arms of strangers. They lovingly, sometimes

The Christmas of Childhood

awkwardly, hold us and point to colorful things and press many toys into our tiny hands.

And all those presents wrapped in all that colorful paper appear. And the angels and stars and Santa Clauses all speak of different realities beyond what we have come to "know" and feel familiar with.

Some of us experience our first long-distance travels to visit grandparents. Long car rides or plane rides give us new impressions. We may experience an entirely new location, and different energies, in another part of the country. Perhaps we experience a city or the country for the first time.

As babies we experience these changes without forming articulated images, but deep neurochemical and sensory memories are formed. We really need simple images, experiences and energies at Christmas time. More in the mood of a humble stable than the mood of Toys-R-Us.

You may want to check your own baby book, look at old photos or speak with your parents or other relatives to ask about your first Christmas? Look at the changes of Christmas and imagine being a baby. We don't have specific memories, but chances are you hold deep impressions about your first Christmas.

I was the first child and my parents were thrilled with their little infant daughter. I have photos of my father holding me in his arms in front of the Christmas tree. Somehow I have a deep felt sense of being surrounded with love and joy based on a few photos. At the same time I am aware of my deep, subtle anxieties about Christmas. Like many, my Christmas feelings are paradoxical and feel so much a part of my being, a sign of early biographical origin.

What about your feelings? Perhaps your parents found new parenting and the demands of the holiday stressful. Perhaps you were a highly sensitive baby. Perhaps your first Christmas was too much to absorb and you felt uncomfortable and over-stimulated.

Think back in time, sense back in time, to your beginning. What do you feel about your very first Christmas? How old were you? Old enough to pull the wrapping off a present? Or were you still a newborn held closely by your mother or father? Did you have siblings filled with Christmas excitement and jealousy of the new baby?

How do your thoughts right now create new feelings about the Christmas you create for yourself? How do you perceive the Christmas

The Christmas of Childhood

experience of your children or your grandchildren? How would you like them to experience Christmas with the understanding of creating a nurturing balance of stimulation and calming?

OUR SECOND CHRISTMAS

By our second Christmas most of us are pretty mobile—crawling or walking. We are anywhere between just turning one or almost 2—a huge range in child development. We have the ability to use our hands to grab and hold, rip and pry, push and pull. Christmas is a time of temptation, of delight and probably, of danger.

There are many things to touch and many things to taste (so much seems to fit into our mouths). There may be lots of sweets that taste good but over tax our biology (and produce sticky hands that annoyingly, must be washed). Perhaps this Christmas primarily stimulates touch and taste. Visually there may be too much to focus on causing all the images to blur together.

Consider how Christmas surprises us. A tree suddenly appears in the house. Imagine that—a tree in the house! And it is full of funny little things and lots of colors. Lots of sparkly lights are hanging everywhere, so much to reach for with our pudgy little hands. For those of us who are social and outgoing, we have a great deal of fun, up to the point when our systems break down with over-stimulation and exhaustion. For those of us who are shy and sensitive, we may feel overwhelm. If overwhelmed, we may cry, get agitated or simply shut down and fall asleep. If our parents are relaxed, we may be encouraged to have an exciting and comfortable Christmas. If our parents are tense and anxious, we may be taught that Christmas is dangerous and demanding. How different this second Christmas can be for us.

This is also the Christmas that the funny man with the red suit and the white beard makes an impact on our picture of Christmas. We are told we must sit in his lap while our mother takes our picture. Is this fun?

Our parents may read us Christmas stories. Maybe about a baby that was born a long time ago with lots of animals around. Or we might learn that something amazing happens on the "night before Christmas" when the funny man in the red suit comes down our chimney. We don't really understand either story but our parents seem to feel these stories are very special.

Most of all our parents want us to have a

perfect Christmas. There is so much going on as they prepare for the holiday. They may be hopeful and happy or anxious and stressed. We absorb all their feelings and reflect their moods. We certainly get excited and maybe a little cranky.

Then one morning so many boxes appear. After we rip off the paper wrapping, we find a new toy, and another toy, and another toy, and another toy... So much choice and stimulation. Pictures and videos are being taken. Mommy and Daddy and our siblings are so animated and lively.

Then we must dress-up and go to another house where there are more presents, people and food. The day is endless.

A few days later, the tree is gone and the house is different.

How do you imagine your second Christmas? It is easy to get a sense of how Christmas imprints and impresses our being. We have sensory, emotional and energetic experiences that begin to create our relationship to Christmas. Most likely we do not have a store of distinct visual and auditory memories but the foundation on which we build the Christmas of Childhood is firmly constructed in our early Christmases.

Our Third Christmas

Something very important happens around our third Christmas. We say "I" for the first time. This is a developmental miracle. We feel and name our selfhood. "I" is the only word that means something different to everyone who speaks it. Saying "I" is like placing the star on top of the Christmas tree—a very little tree.

Because of the awakened but naive sense of "I," our third Christmas is the first where we ever so slightly step back and observe. Christmas begins to have something to do with us. We pick up that our parents are creating a magical time focused on our feelings of surprise and delight. We begin to have a dreamy paradoxical sense of our own importance and our own powerlessness. This is the beginning of our Christmas angst.

Those of us who like intense stimulation, love the excitement and the attention. We delight in the growing anticipation and can hardly wait for Christmas morning. We love the fantasy and the surreal quality of the day. We move from toy to toy with delight. We are not affected by the holiday tension and anxieties in our parents. Christmas is fun, the best day of the year.

The Christmas of Childhood

A few of us, who react to the moods of our parents and don't deal well with excitement and stimulation find Christmas overwhelming, are now able to retreat by ourselves. All the toys are wonderful but we tend to choose one toy to focus on and often find a calm corner to safely play with it. We struggle with getting dressed up and sitting at the table with all the special foods. Perhaps we wonder why our older sibling or cousin seems so happy, when that's not what we feel. Christmas and all the activity are too much to manage.

If we are in a family that is religious, this Christmas is the first Christmas when the Baby Jesus gets our attention with some naive understanding. We are told that Christmas is about this baby. Perhaps we wonder why this baby is so important. We have a baby brother or sister and find a baby is pretty boring. Yet, despite our sense of our sibling, the mysterious meaning of the Nativity is dawning in our souls.

From Santa Claus to the Baby Jesus, our third Christmas awakens mixed feelings and many vague questions about Christmas. The feelings and questions reappear with each subsequent Christmas.

Again, much of the impact of your third

Christmas depends on several realities: how old you are, how many siblings you have and their ages, how sensitive you are and how social you are. I was just two years old, my sister was not yet born. I was very sensitive to my parents' mood and very social. I loved visual images so the fantasy of the decorations was wonderful—especially the tinsel. I have always been drawn to spiritual and religious meaning and symbols (and babies) and found the Nativity story very special. On the other side of Christmas, even today I feel a "curled-up-in-Daddy's-lap" cuddliness when I hear the words, "Twas the night before Christmas..."

Both my parents loved creating perfect images. I, their precious and precocious two-year old, was the central part and focus of their perfect Christmas image. Both my parents were bipolar and found Christmas a time of mania. As an adult I would always imitate their needs and try to create the perfect Christmas. I never thought about Christmas as a calming and centering time of the year. I wanted a Christmas that looked like a photograph in a magazine and I did everything (except bake cookies). This was such an instinctual drive in me—truly a mirror of my early Christmases.

What was your experience? Were you secure in your family? Were you sensitive to the mood changes of your parents at Christmas? If you look at your feelings about Christmas today, how do you imagine your third Christmas shaped those feelings?

OUR FOURTH CHRISTMAS

During your fourth Christmas, you are anywhere from just three years old to almost four years old. You are on the threshold between toddlerhood and childhood. You have a good grasp of language, your physical coordination is strong, your likes and dislikes are clear.

If you are a "thinker" the fourth Christmas is the Christmas of questions, questions, questions. If you are a physical type, this is the Christmas of energetic activity, which may cause trouble. If you are a feeling perceptive child, this is the Christmas of growing imaginations inspired by lights, colors, smells, music and magic. Your mood is now becoming a response to the season, and not just a reaction to your parents' moods and expectations.

If you are closer to four years old on December 25th, your fourth Christmas is also the Christmas when you start making a list of what you want. The idea of Christmas gifts and wishes has awakened in you. More importantly, the specter of disappointment has taken hold of your soul. For many the idea of deserving or not deserving what you desire begins to have significance. Who can forget the haunting lyrics of "Santa Claus is Coming to Town."

You better watch out, you better not cry
Better not pout, I'm telling you why
Santa Claus is comin' to town
He's making a list and checking it twice
Gonna find out who's naughty and nice
Santa Claus is comin to town
He sees you when you're sleepin'
He knows when you're a wake
He knows if you've been bad or good
So be good for goodness sake
Oh! You better watch out, you better not cry
Better not pout, I'm telling you why
Santa Claus is comin' to town

During the fourth Christmas, a part of the holiday becomes a bit sinister. Christmas becomes a tool of behavioral blackmail or punishment. We no longer feel our simple presence merits the joys and gifts of Christmas, we must

The Christmas of Childhood

earn it by being "nice." The Christmas of Childhood by the fourth Christmas, becomes a training ground for good behavior. How do you feel this aspect of your early Christmas experience shapes your Christmas feelings?

Santa Claus, the great bringer of presents, is now a big deal,. Santa is a wonderful story that parents eagerly share and elaborate. Sadly, it is also a lie that in a few years is revealed and can cause confusion and disturbance. I know a number of adults who talk about the difficulty of dealing with the emotional blow of learning that their parents were *lying*. We all need to consider the impact of discovering our parents' Christmas lies in our own biographies and how it plays in our current Christmas feelings. Do we feel there is a "lie" living in any or all of the meanings of Christmas?

Here are some additional questions to reflect on as you consider your fourth Christmas: Did you like the cold weather? Were you allowed to help decorate the tree or did your parents do the tree while you were asleep one night? Did you have traditional visits with your extended family? Did you love seeing cousins, grandparents, etc. If your parents were unhappy or divorced how did this shape your holidays? Did you go to

Christmas services at your church? What were your family traditions? Do you maintain these traditions still?

THE FIRST CHRISTMAS SHADOWS

Growing older, even being four or five, changes our view of Christmas. Christmas shadows begin to appear. We have begun to want and not want. And we begin to sense that Christmas magic doesn't happen magically. We start to see all the work it takes to create even the simplest aspects of the Christmas of Childhood. We also become more consciously sensitive to the dynamics of family life stressed by the demands of this holiday. This is when the bright, colorful and wonderful Child's Christmas begins to cast dark shadows. These shadows shape our adult Christmas nightmares and we try to avoid them in all our future Christmases.

The Christmas of Childhood floods our souls with dreams, hopes, and excitement along with the shadows of disappointment, envy, and resentment. The deep and complex emotions we feel about Christmas are often rooted in our early holiday memories.

Christmas speaks to the child and to the emotions in every soul. We seem to feel it is the

The Christmas of Childhood

time of year devoted to generosity, abundance and specialness. Christmas is a time beyond the ordinary. As very young children, we float between two worlds: Our child's world of innocence and wonder and the world of adults with logic and consequence. Christmas is a time when the very young child finds her parents have entered into her world of magic.

Our nascent senses are innocent and eager. We can find total delight and absorption in a taste, smell, color, form, reflection or texture. With the sensory pageantry of Christmas we are flooded with impressions of all kinds. If we adults were to experience Christmas with the naïve senses of the child who is somewhere between birth and walking and talking, we would feel we had taken a hallucinogenic drug. The sensory excitement and wonder of a child is so open compared to the sensory inhibition and wisdom of an adult.

On top of these early, perhaps buried, experiences add your later childhood and adolescent Christmases. What memories from your Christmases between 6 and 16 stand out in your soul? How do these memories, the good and the bad, impact your present Christmas? What was it like to not just receive presents, but to also give presents? How did Christmas appear in your friendships? In your first romantic relationships?

CHRISTMAS, DIVORCE AND DEATH

Did your family break apart through divorce or death? How did loss and separation impact your Christmas feelings and images? How do we integrate grief, fear, and rage into this holiday of love, peace and joy? Christmas is the holiday of light, but some of us experience only darkness for one or more Christmases.

If your parents were divorced, Christmas becomes divided. For some, two Christmas are better than one and for others the Christmases after divorce are incredibly difficult. If you have a blended family through a parent's remarriage, how did you blend different holiday traditions? I remember a Christmas with my step-mother's family. It was at her sister's home with all my step-cousins. My step-aunt had presents for all the children, except me. It was a Cinderella Christmas with no fairy godmother. I still feel pain over 50 years later.

Growing Up in a Home
Without Christmas

Four or five is the age when those of us who for religious or cultural reasons do not have Christmas with our families begin to be aware that other families have an important celebration filled with gifts and food, decorations and music in late December. Even when the whole world seems to have this magical holiday, we don't. Children without Christmas, can't help but wonder about, and perhaps even envy or resent, those who celebrate Christmas.

I have a friend who was the only Jewish kid in her class in elementary school. Her feelings were not considered by her classmates, her teachers or her parents. Now married to a Christian, she has a lovely little girl. In spite of very ecumenical spiritual feelings and a well-articulated relationship to Christ (though not to Christianity), she cannot tolerate Christmas in her home.

If you did not celebrate Christmas in your home, what were your feelings about it? What were you taught about Christmas and the people who celebrated Christmas?

If you are not Christian, why do you now

celebrate Christmas? How does this relate to you childhood sense of Christmas?

The Christmas of Selfhood

The Christmas
of Selfhood

The celebrations of Christmas have moved from the vast world of nature to the intimate world of your home, from your relationship to the birth of Jesus to your relationships with others, and finally from your dreams of your childhood to your dreams of your selfhood.

The final Christmas to contemplate is the Christmas of Selfhood. This Christmas is just dawning in your consciousness. Beginning with a longing, a soft inner cry for something beyond the other five Christmases, the Christmas of Selfhood is rising in your soul like the sun on a misty Christmas morning. In the cyclical flow, at Christmas time our souls are filled with and open to the invisible world of Spirit, all the glories of the heavens.

A YEARLY JOURNEY

The Christmas of Selfhood calls for a state of consciousness that evolves from a deep wintry sleep into a warming dream of self-awareness and finally toward a new waking imagination of your own soul development. Deeply personal and deeply spiritual in its celebration, gifts, and meaning, the Christmas of Selfhood asks you to follow your own inner path once a year.

This path feels like a journey to the manger in your soul, the place in your soul where the divine in you is reborn each year. You find your soul's expression of divinity evolving. In the soul's manger you find a new perspective on your individuality as both a spiritual being and an earthly being.

INNER AND INDIVIDUAL

No one shares this Christmas of Selfhood with you. Nor can you experience another's journey to their soul's manger. The Christmas of Selfhood is the solitary Christmas. Joyfully solitary.

Like the Sun in the Christmas of Nature, which at each Winter Solstice remains the same sun but carries different forces from the Zodiac, each Christmas your "I Am," the Divine within, moves into a new experience of selfhood. The gifts of new strengths and new challenges found in the Christmas of Selfhood offer the form and force for your soul's creative activity in the coming year.

The blessings revealed in your soul's manger nourish and nurture the courage in your heart and the imagination in your desires. As the Christmas of Riches delights your senses, the Christmas of Selfhood delights your inner being. You find your soul illuminated with new lights of transcendent truth, beauty, harmony, and goodness.

Each year you find in the manger a new way of being in your thinking, in your feeling, and in your willing. You find a personal star that shines your way to a reconnection to your higher self and guides you to a year of practical and moral fulfillment. You experience an inner Christmas of Nativity.

The Christmas of Selfhood mirrors the Christmas of Relationships. From the manger of your soul you relate to and embrace all the many aspects of your inner life. You will be introduced for the first time to parts of your soul that are just emerging. You will say goodbye with sadness and gratitude to the parts of your inner life that are fading.

With tenderness, you recall the complex memories of the past year and shape the dreams of the coming year. The inner gestures of recollection and anticipation, of self-celebration

The Christmas of Selfhood

and self-evolution, of self-forgiveness and self-encouragement are the gifts of the Christmas of Selfhood.

How do you celebrate The Christmas of Selfhood? There are many ways. Most important is the need to spend some quiet time alone. Take a long, slow walk with yourself or find a quiet place to sit by yourself. No iPods or cell-phones. You want to give yourself sacred silence with no distractions.

Imagine going into the purest and most powerful place of your being. From this place ask yourself questions and listen to your answers. You may want to use a special Christmas Journal to write down your questions and answers.

Your Christmas of Selfhood requires more than one day of celebration and attention. Please consider 3,4,7 or 12 days of celebration. Twelve is the ideal number of days because it symbolizes the circle of life and completion, but twelve may require too much commitment for you. Commit to a number of days that is just beyond your sense of comfort and capacity. It is in the extra attention that you will open up the gift of Selfhood.

You don't need to spend more than 10-30 minutes celebrating each day. Choose or create a meditative verse to open and close your celebration.

You can choose to meditate on a question or on an image. Work with the question or image twice: once to see what appears as self-awareness in the present, then again, with the goal of inspiring a new possibility. Selfhood seeks to strengthen will, the intentional force that allows us to become more fully ourselves and express ourselves spiritually and practically. Do not confuse this will imagination with creating a "to do" list or a "to transform" list. It is a lighting of an inner spark to illumine and warm your way in the coming year.

In my *Inner Christmas* messages (to which I hope you are subscribed—www.innerchristmas.com), I work with a yearly theme to guide each daily meditation of the Christmas of Selfhood. If you are not interested in my guiding messages or a self determined theme of meditation, you can also simply quiet your mind and see what comes to the surface.

I find it very strengthening and deepening to write during these meditations. So I urge you to keep a Selfhood journal. You can do a writing meditation, where you record all your thoughts as they surface in your mind. Another writing

The Christmas of Selfhood

activity is the recording of the feelings that arise after the meditation.

The celebration of the Christmas of Selfhood is yours to create and fulfill. You can include or leave out whatever feels right. Just celebrate the unfolding deed of love that is YOU.

Celebrating Christmas! Celebrating You!

Until recent times, the Christmas season was a time for stimulation. Winter was a time of little activity and human souls needed the celebrations to reengage with life. This was true for all the festivals and holidays. The routine of daily life was relieved by joyful and boisterous rituals and revelries.

Today modern souls need to find a new way to celebrate Christmas. Our daily lives are much too stimulating year around—stillness and simplicity are not part of our lives. Quite the contrary, we suffer from the busyness of life. Our senses are bombarded with sights and sounds. Agitation and anxiety disturb our souls. We need our festivals and holidays to restore peace to our hearts.

In particular, the festival of Christmas needs to be a time of calming and centering activity. The insights into the six ways your soul finds meaning in Christmas guide you to celebrating Christmas in calming, enriching, ensouling

The Christmas of Selfhood

ways. You can find the spiritual depth and significance of the cosmic Christmases of Nature and Nativity. You can find the sensuous pleasure and warm connection of the social Christmases of Riches and Relationships. You can find the healing, self-awareness and empowering direction for your future in the personal Christmases of Childhood and Selfhood.

Christmas is the time of year when your soul can reconnect with the meaning, significance and purpose of the cosmos, humanity, and yourself. The Christmas holiday lives in your soul to bring renewal, restoration and resolve to your thinking, feeling and willing. Christmas brings joy and wisdom to your life.

May all your Christmas Celebrations be blessed.

More from Lynn Jericho
Available Soon

The following books will soon be available to further support your experience of Christmas:

Six Ways To Celebrate Christmas! & Celebrate You! Working Journal
for Healing, Liberating and Strengthening Your Christmas Experience

Work with your responses to the many self-reflective questions found in *Six Ways To Celebrate Christmas! & Celebrate You!* Additional thoughts and questions are included.

Apply the wisdom in the 3 'R's of education: reading, 'riting, 'rithmetic. First, you read to inspire thoughts and feelings, then you 'rite them down and let them expand. Then you find the freedom of inner 'rithmetic where you add, subtract, divide and multiply your Christmas meanings.

When you bring your attention to your thoughts and feelings and clarify them enough to write them down, you find they open up to the light of consciousness. Journal-writing nurtures and empowers your work of inner development.

Inner Christmas
A Guide to Celebrating the Christmas of Selfhood during the Twelve Holy Nights

Learn the mysteries of the Twelve Holy Nights and why they offer your inner life the deepest possibility for psychospiritual development every year. Find creative inspirations for designing your Christmas of Selfhood. This inspiring little book will bring clarity, warmth and authenticity to your unfolding inner life and new meaning to your Christmases.

Inner Christmas is a yearly ritual of giving birth to a new sense of self.

The Twelve Soul Qualities
Inner Christmas Meditations for the Twelve Holy Nights and the Rest of the Inner Year

Every year Lynn Jericho sends out a daily e-message during the Twelve Holy Nights between December 25 and January 6. The messages work within a theme and are under 1000 words.

The Twelve Soul Qualities is a beautifully expanded version of Inner Christmas 2007. Nurture your soul's qualities of receptivity, generosity, humility, nobility, fluidity, solidity, luminosity, reflectivity, equanimity, fecundity, sagacity, and unity.

Each study of a soul quality offers original insight and inspiring questions to support the richness of your inner life.

To learn more about these books and to purchase a copy for yourself or your family and friends visit www.innerchristmas.com.

Appendix:
De-Clutter Your Holidays

DETERMINE HOLIDAY CLUTTER

Holiday clutter develops when we follow traditions out of boring habit, shallow sentimentality or retail seduction. Our holidays often end up cluttered with meaningless stuff. Magazines and shops seduce us into feeling we must add to our holiday experience. Obviously many people spend money, and make money, expanding and inflating holiday traditions. We head to the store and not to our hearts to bring new richness to our celebrations.

How do we get rid of holiday clutter? How do we create elegant holidays? Elegant means graceful and simple. Can we balance the materialism of our holidays with some self-awareness and spiritual attention to our sense of the meaning living in our traditions?

BE CAREFUL

I must make a confession. Years ago I was moving with my children to a new home. Packing up a household is always a good time to clear out and de-clutter but it must be done wisely. Finding the boxes of Christmas decorations brought back all the ancient history colored by divorce and, especially the lonely nights trying to make the perfect Christmas celebration. In a gesture of careless liberation, I threw out all the boxes. However among all the decorations that had no meaning, there were some that held special significance and emotional continuity. I had tossed out the meaningful with the meaningless. I was foolish.

Finding the Real Meaning of Your Traditions

The questions below will help you sort through your traditions, to help you connect deeply with the meaningful. They support you in recognizing what is merely holiday clutter. These questions can guide the choices you make in enriching your holidays with new traditions.

If you go through three or four of the 12 questions with three traditions, you will find a new level of discernment and holiday joy living in your soul. You will find yourself naturally grasping the meaning living or lacking in all your traditions. Ask family members what their feelings about the traditions are. Invite a few friends over to a pre-Halloween (or Thanksgiving, Chanukah, or Christmas) tea and use these questions to share traditions and inspire insight.

You might find most of your traditions have heartfelt meaning for you and your family, but there are just too many of them. You can divide up your traditions into three groups—the extra-special group that must be part of every year, the traditions for the odd years and the traditions for the even years.

I have designed the questions around the Twelve Senses described by Rudolf Steiner, the founder of Waldorf Education. Our perceptions of and sensitivities to all the varied aspects of our holiday traditions are the source of our joy and our difficulties. The nature of the questions will give you a sense of each holy, soul-shaping sense.

Holidays are holy days ... and are most joyful when they make our consciousness more awake to the holy in our lives. Traditions provide us an empowered sense of the sacred. De-clutter your holidays and give your soul a more joyful and meaningful experience.

If you have any questions or insights to share please email Lynn Jericho at lynnjericho@gmail.com. More insights into the personal holiness of holidays can be found at www.innerchristmas.com. Sign up to receive the 12 daily inspirations during the Twelve Holy Nights this Christmas.

TOUCH

Does this tradition wrap my soul with special feelings? Does this tradition push against my material life with deep spiritual symbolism? Or does it represent the positive or negative impact of materialism on my soul life?

WELL-BEING

Does this tradition restore my soul, feed my soul, comfort my soul? Does it enliven my holiday with delight, depth or devotion?

Appendix

Movement

What is the goal or purpose of this tradition? Does the tradition bring me to a inner stillness or to a new movement in my soul?

Balance

Does this tradition create a balance between spirit and matter? How does it create spiritual or emotional freedom for me?

Smell

Does this tradition still have inner freshness for me? Or is it musty and old? What are the memories that this tradition brings into intimate connection with me?

Taste

Sweet: Does this tradition bring me sweetness and make my life free of suffering – even for only a moment?

Sour: Does this tradition wake me up to things I might forget or not notice?

Salty: Does this tradition crystalize an inner experience of the divine for my soul? Does it crystalize beautiful memories?

Bitter: Does this tradition heal a pain or suffering? Does it bring a lesson?

Yuk: Does this tradition lack all meaning – giving you a "yuk" experience? Is it in bad taste to continue with this tradition?

VISION

Does this tradition color my soul and brighten my sense of the holy? Does it illuminate the shadows of my soul? Does it focus on the meaning of the holiday?

WARMTH

Does this tradition take the chill from my heart? Do I let the warmth of this tradition permeate my soul? Why do I experience this tradition as warming?

HEARING

Does this tradition offer sounds that stir my being? Does it bring harmonious music to my relationships?

WORD SENSE

What are the single words or phrases that come to mind about this tradition? Does it represent a simple gesture or form that shapes a meaningful holiday?

THOUGHT SENSE

What are the ideas and the ideals behind the traditions that I love? Is there a story behind the tradition?

SENSE OF THE TRUE BEING OF OTHERS

What is the true authentic being of those I share this tradition with? How does each tradition give me a truer sense of these individuals?

Appendix

My Note of Gratitude

My heart is full of gratitude for all the wonderful people that have supported and encouraged me as I have put together this book. As I think about them, I feel my whole being smiling.

I would like to name all of them, but it would take longer to write than the book as I would drift into a reverie of thoughts about each one. Perhaps one day I will post on my website a gratitude page with all the names and descriptions of the love they gave me. What a happy idea.

To all my subscribers, many who have been with me for years, I want to say thank you.

There are three people whose generosity of time and talent has been extraordinary. They made the book happen.

Catharine Clarke

Alan Shalleck

John Beck

All three of them are wonderful writers working on important books of their own. They took time away from their own creative efforts to edit, design and produce my work. Words fail the love and gratitude I feel.

Two individuals bless my life always—my daughter, Thea, and my son, Luc. I love you.

Finally, I want to acknowledge Rudolf Steiner (1861-1925). His living wisdom about all things spiritual and material is the inspirational foundation on which my thoughts form. Steiner wrote a verse that I have held in my heart since I first heard it in 1987. In gratitude I share it with you.

> *The soul's questings are quickening,*
> *The wills deeds are waxing,*
> *And life's fruits grow ripe.*
>
> *I feel my destiny.*
> *My destiny finds me.*
> *I feel my star.*
> *My star finds me.*
> *I feel my goals.*
> *My goals find me.*
>
> *My soul and the world are but one.*
>
> *Life becomes brighter about me.*
> *Life becomes harder for me.*
> *Life becomes richer within me.*

My Note of Gratitude

Lynn Jericho was a Christmas baby.

December 11, 1947, two weeks before Christmas, I am born. My birth announcement is a Christmas card. Every year my parents put up our Christmas tree on my birthday. As a little girl I find Christmas simple and magical. Then Santa Claus becomes a fantasy and Christmas becomes a confusion of the  secular and the sacred. My Christmas moods range from delight to disappointment. From my early teens, I begin to feel there is something missing.

December, 1986, as a parent in the Princeton Waldorf school, I hear about the Twelve Holy  Nights. Rudolf Steiner, the founder of Waldorf education and extraordinary visionary and source of mystical wisdom, brought many insights on the yearly festivals. He revealed the Twelve Holy Nights between Christmas and Epiphany as the time when the Spirit of the individual and the Spiritual World are most connected. It is a time for special attention to our inner path of personal development. I begin to explore a variety of intentional practices. I don't succeed as I forget to pay attention or choose readings that fail to lead me into myself. Yet, I continue to feel there is something of deep possibility during these nights. Years go by.

On **December 23, 2004**, I find myself at Rockefeller Center, looking at the giant tree with its thousands of lights and listening to canned Christmas Carols. A great New York experience but so electric and commercial. I come home and write an email to the several hundred people on my mailing list about the meaning of Christmas and the Twelve Holy Nights. Spontaneously, I commit to sending a daily message between December 25 and January 6. Over the next two days I decide to write about the 12 senses - the ways we perceive ourselves, the world and other human beings. Christmas morning I write and send out my first message. I include a thoughtful description of the perception and a few questions for self-reflection. I am scared - what if people find it silly? People don't. I get emails thanking me. People forward it to friends. I keep writing every day.

In **June, 2005**, Eric Utne, founder of *Utne* magazine, sends me an email, asking if I will do a piece on the Twelve Holy Nights for his great *Cosmo Doogood's Urban Almanac, 2006*. Of course! 50000 copies are printed. It is a gem of an almanac.

December, 2005. I send out another Christmas message and promise another set of daily messages. This time I work with prepositions. Why prepositions? Because prepositions indicate relationship. We can learn a lot about how we relate to our personal lives if we contemplate prepositions like *in, between, toward, over,* etc.

Again, the messages are well-received. I realize that I have found a wonderful way to celebrate the Holy Nights and that the gifts I offer have meaning for most people. I begin to think of doing a book called *Inner Christmas.*

August, 2006. Inspiration strikes. I have received a number of short flash movies promoting coaching services or inspirational books. Why not create an *Inner Christmas* movie that would bring images, words and music about the mystery of the Twelve Holy Nights to viewers? I buy the software and engage the support of my dear friend, Catharine, and my partner, Alan. I choose the images and write the text and production begins.

December 18, 2006. The release date is December 1, but due to technical difficulties The Inner Christmas Movie is sent to 223 individuals on December 18. By January 6, over 30,000 people in 70 countries have viewed the movie and 10,000 have subscribed to the messages. I get notes from all over the world. The 2006 Holy Nights messages are about Soul Qualities, core experiences of our inner life.

December, 2008. Inner Christmas continues to grow. More and more subscribers sign up.

All this is amazing. It is joyful and thrilling and a huge responsibility. But I have the Christmas I always longed for.

The rest of the year, I am an integrative wisdom counselor who helps people heal and grow. You can learn more about my life and my work at **www.lynnjericho.com**. I also give talks and workshops on personal development and sometimes on esoteric spiritual topics.

Photo of Lynn Jericho by Sokol Kokoshi.

%

Original photography for some chapter images from members of stock.xchng *at* sxc.hu:
p.34: leovdworp; *p.97:* rrss; *p.120* theao211.

%

The nativity image p.48 is based on a 15th c. painting by Dirck Bouts the elder (view at Web Gallery of Art wga.hu*).*

%

Layout: John Beck, Adobe InDesign CS4
Typefaces: Adobe Warnock Pro, Adobe Brioso Pro